Leadership is the capacity to translate vision into reality.
Warren Bennis

Winning at Leading:

A Critical Guide to Effective Leadership and Administration

Nicholas Robertson and Valentine Rodney

Edited by Danielle Brown-Robertson

WINNING AT LEADING: A CRITICAL GUIDE TO EFFECTIVE LEADERSHIP AND (New Ed.) Copyright © 2023 by **Impact Online Institute Global.**

Published by:

Reason with Robdon

ISBN: 978-1-990266-07-2

Book Cover Design by: **Iconic Presence**

- All rights reserved soley by the author. No part of the book may be reproduced, stored in a retreival system or transmitted by any means (mechanical, electronic, photocopy, recording or otherwise) without the written permission of the author.

- All scriptures are taken from the Holy Bible, New Living Translation, copyright ©1996, 2004, 2007 by the Tyndale House Foundation. Used by permission of Tyndale House Publishers Inc., Carol Stream, IL 30188. All rights reserved.

- All definitions are taken from Vine's Expository Dictionary of Old and New Testament Words, copyright © 1997 by Thomas Neilson, Inc. Used by permission of Thomas Neilson Inc., Nashville, Tennessee. All rights reserved.

IOBI instructors are available to speak and provide training at your conferences, workshops, crusades, conventions, seminars, youth ministry, mentorship, men's ministry, couple's ministry and any other ministry engagement.

School's Contact Details:

Email:	iobi@positivevibrationglobal.com
Website:	https://www.positivevibrationglobal.com/impact-online-bible-institute
Follow us: FB, IG, YT, Twitter	Reason with Robdon/ Impact Online Bible Institute/BuildAman Foundation Global

TABLE OF CONTENTS

TABLE OF CONTENTS 5
ACKNOWLEDGMENT 7
WINNING AT LEADING 8
QUALITIES OF A GOOD LEADER 18
QUALITIES OF A GOOD LEADER 27
QUALITIES OF A GOOD LEADER 30
THE HEART OF LEADERSHIP 44
PREPARING TO MORROW'S LEADERS 53
CHOOSING THE MOST EFFECTIVE LEADERSHIP STYLE 57
CHOOSING THE MOST EFFECTIVE LEADERSHIP STYLE 63
CHOOSING THE MOST EFFECTIVE LEADERSHIP STYLE 68
CHOOSING THE MOST EFFECTIVE LEADERSHIP STYLE 73
CHOOSING THE MOST EFFECTIVE LEADERSHIP STYLE 77
CHOOSING THE MOST EFFECTIVE LEADERSHIP STYLE 81
CHOOSING THE MOST EFFECTIVE LEADERSHIP STYLE .... 83DEVELOP AN ACTION PLAN 91
PLAN WITH AN OUTCOME IN MIND 103

MOBILISATING THE TEAM 109
LEADERSHIP AND MANAGEMENT 127
LEADERSHIP AND ACCOUNTABILITY 135
LEADERSHIP AND ACCOUNTABILITY 143
LEADERSHIP AND ACCOUNTABILITY 147
LEADERSHIP AND ACCOUNTABILITY 153
.... 158
LEADERSHIP, PROFESSIONAL &SPIRITUAL
DEVELOPMENT 158
LEADERSHIP AND CHANGE 163
LEADERSHIP CHARACTER AND INTEGRITY . 169
DEMONSTRATING AND PRESERVING
INTEGRITY 175
PRAYER AND LEADERSHIP 182
THE LEADERSHIP, GOD'S WORD, AND THE
CHURCH 195
THE LEADER AND THE HOLY SPIRIT 207
NOW, WIN AT LEADING 216
GLOSSARY 225
REFERENCE 226

ACKNOWLEDGMENT

Writing a book of this magnitude is not something that is done every day, but "WINNING AT LEADING: A CRITICAL GUIDE: Guide to Effective Leadership and Administration" was an exciting journey for us. We enjoyed every moment of the process as our passion is to help believers better apply the scriptures. God has given us the talent and ability to write, we would therefore like to thank Him first and foremost. Without His leadership, wisdom, strength and help, this book would only be still a thought.

Secondly, we would like to thank Danielle Robertson for her invaluable contribution to this project.

We would also like to say a big thank you to Oneil Brown from Iconic Presence for designing the book cover. It is attractive and one can truly judge this book by its cover.

WINNING AT LEADING

"Success will not lower its standard to us. We must raise our standard to success."
— *Rev. Randall R. McBride,* Jr.

Winning at leadership is not the outcome of waving a magic wand; neither is it the product of chance or an act of mystery. It is an approach to leadership that requires us to skillfully adapt the appropriate leadership style to influence others to maximise their input to attain a goal. The successful attainment of an objective is best achieved through the collective efforts of a group of individuals who share a common focus; they are often referred to as a team. The team leader must be able to inspire the members to work collectively towards a vision with excellence.

Therefore, the leader plays a critical role in deriving and communicating the vision with others, directing them toward the goal.

Leadership is more about influence than achievements, although successful attainments can become an asset in fulfilling the task at hand. Throughout history, humans have differed in perspective on the characteristics that amount to outstanding leadership. This sometimes contradicts even what the sovereign God considers essential to leadership. In the Bible, Samuel, one of Israel's judges was tasked by God to anoint Israel's second king, one contrary to his own liking, thus he did not see David as the suitable candidate for king.

So it happened, when they had come, he looked at Eliab [the eldest son] and thought, "Surely the Lord's anointed is before Him." But the Lord said to Samuel, "Do not look at his appearance or at the height of his stature, because I have rejected him. *For the Lord sees not as man sees; for man looks at the outward appearance, but the Lord looks at the heart." Then Jesse called Abinadab and had him pass before Samuel. But Samuel said, "The Lord has not chosen this one either." Next Jesse had Shammah pass by. And Samuel said, "The Lord has not chosen him either." Jesse had seven of his sons pass before Samuel. But Samuel said to Jesse, "The Lord has not chosen [any of] these." Then Samuel said to Jesse, "Are all your sons here?" Jesse replied, "There is still one left, the youngest; he is tending the sheep." Samuel said to Jesse, "Send word and bring him; because we will not sit down [to eat the sacrificial meal] until he comes here." So, Jesse sent word and brought him in. Now he had a ruddy complexion, with beautiful eyes and a handsome appearance. The Lord said [to Samuel], "Arise, anoint him; for this is he." Then Samuel took the horn of oil and anointed David in the presence of his brothers; and the Spirit of the Lord came mightily upon David from that day forward.* **(1 Samuel 16:6-13, AMP)**

Leadership is more than physical appearance or strength; it has to do with character. Individuals have no control over their height, age, and in some instances, size. David was ruddy but this did not deter his ability to lead Israel.

Through education, experience, and training, one can develop his/her attitude, skills, and conduct. We can best see a person's character through their commitment, loyalty, passion, drive, and relationship with God, all of which form the basis for God's choice. God rejected Eliab: *"Don't judge by his appearance or height, for I have rejected him. The Lord doesn't see things the way you see them. People judge by outward appearance, but the Lord looks at the heart."*

(1 Samuel 16:17)

Winning at leading requires a leader of excellent character, that is, a person who is dependable, trustworthy, sincere, loyal, and most importantly, a pursuer of God's will. The leader is the steward of

God's work and people. Therefore, he/she must completely submit to God and His will and maintain an excellent line of communication with Him. Let us think of God as an army general who is not only privy to details about the mission, but He is the orchestrator of the mission. He has the critical information necessary for the successful execution of the task. The leader (platoon commander) leading the troops into the mission, is limited in his/her knowledge and, therefore, must enter several mission briefings (prayer) to discuss God's expectations. In these meetings, God advises him/her of the most effective approach. As he/she talks with God, they develop their interpersonal skills. Undoubtably, leading people can be disheartening at times. This was quite evident in the discourse of the exodus leader, Moses, as he poured out his frustration in prayer to God.

The people stood up in the doorways of their tents whining, making the Lord extremely angry. This aggravated Moses to the extent he considered it the judgement of God.

And Moses asked the Lord, "Why are you treating me, your servant, so harshly? Have mercy on me! What did I do to deserve the burden of all these people? Did I give birth to them? Did I bring them into the world? Why did you tell me to carry them in my arms like a mother carries a nursing baby? How can I carry them to the land you swore to give their ancestors? Where am I supposed to get meat for all these people? They keep whining to me, saying, 'Give us meat to eat!' I can't carry all these people by myself! The load is far too heavy! If this is how you intend to treat me, just go ahead, and kill me. Do me a favour and spare me this misery!" **(Numbers 11:11-15)**

The effective leader must be humble enough to depend on God but strong enough to lead God's people. As he/she advances within the mission, regular communication must be made with the control centre (God), seeking advice and permission to engage because the Lord cares.

The Lord directs the steps of the godly. He delights in every detail of their lives. **(Psalms 37:23)**

Whereas the platoon leader's strength, physique, knowledge, and might may be an asset to fulfilling God's mission, it is useless if he/she fails to lead as the chief commander directs. The successful undertaking and completion of a mission is directly correlated to our sincere love, submission, teachable spirit, and our willingness to totally depend upon God. There is distinction between God's choice for leadership and man's selection. In a democratic society people will vote for leaders based on likeable characteristics for example:

- *policies*

- *personalities*
- *political alignment*

This does not always amount to the best outcome because a true leader must follow Him who is omniscient, omnipresent, and omnipotent. Choosing based on external attributes alone can be detrimental and have lasting implications. Israel chose their first king simply because it was the norm among heathen nations to have kings.

Finally, all the elders of Israel met at Ramah to discuss the matter with Samuel. "Look," they told him, "You are now old, and your sons are not like you. Give us a king to judge us like all the other nations have." **(1 Samuel 8:4-5)**

The basis of choosing a leader should not be rooted in earthly motivation but rather the will of God. It is God's desire that we are successful in fulfilling the purpose to which we were sent to earth. The effective leader must see himself helping others to fulfil their purposes while completing God's mission. Jesus' purpose was to save (deliver) His people.

"You are to name him Jesus, for He will save his people from their sins." **(Matthew 1:21)**

However, the mission was wrapped up in His father's will. By fulfilling His purpose, He would fulfill His Father's mission. The father's mission was to establish a lasting relationship with all of humanity.

"For this is how God loved the world: He gave his one and only Son, so that everyone who believes in him will not perish but have eternal life. **(John 3:16)**

What Then Makes a Leader?

A leader is sincerely committed to God's mission and utterly dependent on Him. The leader can inspire and guide others towards fulfilling God's mission while discovering and effectuating purpose. The leader has a clear vision and can communicate this to the team. The leader has the following qualities: wisdom, compassion, love, empathy, temperance, integrity, honesty, courage, and humility. John Maxwell opines, "A leader knows the way, goes the way, and shows the way." The leader must be focused, clearly understand the mission's objectives, be accomplished, and be determined to fulfil the intended tasks. People are more likely to submit to the authority and will of the leader to whom they have confidence. A leader is like a tour guide. People will willingly follow a tour guide because they are confident that the tour director is familiar with the journey to the desired destination. The leader must have the capacity to envision the desired destination and be able to provide information as he/she seeks to guide and motivate the team to the end goal. The leader is the accounting officer to the people he/she leads and is accountable to God.

QUALITIES OF A GOOD LEADER

The Impact of Vision on Leadership

"Quality is never an accident. It is always the result of intelligent effort."

-John Ruskin

The elements of good leadership are:

- *vision,*
- *passion,*
- *integrity.*

In this chapter, we will examine the impact of **vision** on leadership. Later we will examine **passion** and **integrity**.

What is meant by term vision?

A vision is a mental portrait of a preferable future, and it is the perception of the future in reverse, requiring pragmatic steps to be realised.

 **The vision must be well-defined and effectively communicated.**

Dr. Myles Munroe posits "vision is the articulation of the action to get to where the group needs to go." Therefore, the realisation of vision hinges on how clear the message is transmitted to those capable of assisting in the consummation of this foresight. The LORD told the prophet Habakkuk to: *"Write my answer plainly on tablets, so that a runner can carry the correct message to others.*   **(Habakkuk 2:2)**

Here vision derived from the Hebrew word 'chazon' meaning divine communication. Our vision must represent an overview of what God has communicated that is what He hopes to achieve. Don't just coin wishes, listen and record what God desires. Our ideas will always fail; God's desires will be fulfilled.

Many plans are in a man's mind, but it is the LORD'S purpose for him that will stand (be carried out).

(Proverbs 19:21)

Having defined the vision, the leader should record and transform the written ideas into actionable plans to guide the team towards the desired intent. You cannot communicate what is not defined, neither can you inspire people to follow a program that is unclear. The vision serves as the signage constantly providing guidance to the followers and a rubric that allows for frequent evaluation. It helps you to know if you are on course while clarifying the overall expectation. Once written it becomes available for future visits clarifying future uncertainties. It demonstrates how others can help to fulfil the mission. Moving the idea from your mind to paper creates a physical representation of what is to come. Every good vision bears the following qualities:

Elements of a Good Vision

A good vision bares the following qualities:

- It is **given/ revealed** by God. We merely accomplish what God wants. Every inventive idea is first the revelation of the all-knowing God. Jeremiah 29:11 states that God knows the plans He has for us. In Jeremiah 33:3, the write opines "we can call Him and that He will reveal things that we do not know." The writer of Proverbs 3:5-6 reminds us to trust Him, and to acknowledge Him in everything we do. His Word says that He will direct our steps.

- It is **audacious.** The vision must be implausible-beyond what you think is possible or attainable. It constitutes the pinnacle of where you are trying to go and must take you beyond where you are comfortable.

- It is **concise.** The vision should be catchy, short, and easy to remember and repeat. The team members must constantly remind themselves of the overall goal, especially in difficult and uncomfortable seasons.

- It is **built on the competencies of the team.** The base of a compelling vision is the skillset, attitude, strengths, weaknesses, resources, and assets of the visionary and the team.

- It is **clear.** The vision should define the fundamental goal comprehensibly, making it easy for them to understand their roles and contribution to the overall intent. Clarity is important because it provides focus. The instruction to write shifted Habakkuk from being a passive, laid-back hearer to an active, engaged doer. Acting on God's instruction puts us in a position to receive His best.

- It is **a future casting.** The vision is a picture of the future that guides the team's transactional actions informing each step to success. It gives all stakeholders a snapshot of the future, and it shows success in reverse. Writing also helps you to remember what's important. When things are difficult, revisiting the vision will help you stay the course. Writing down the vision spoken to you by God will be a visual reminder of the future success. Matthew 4:1-11 recounts Jesus being tempted by satan: *After 40 days of fasting, the Spirit led Jesus into the wilderness to be tempted by the enemy. Naturally, after 40 days without food, Jesus was hungry. The enemy tempted him three* times. First with bread, then with the pride of proving who He was, and finally with the wealth of the world. Each time Jesus battled the deception of the enemy with 'It is written'.

Jesus was able to revisit the plan and inform His action.

- It is **inspiring**. The vision is a mentally attractive picture that stimulates interest, provokes emotions, fosters enthusiasm, challenges team members, inspires confidence, guides their effort, and manages expectations. Writing also brings a sense of clarity to our thoughts.

- It is **motivating**. The vision provides a mental scaffold that guides the construction of each phase in the dream, directing the team's actions and keeping them in alignment.

- It is **purpose driven.** The vision provides team members with a clear picture of the end goal. The vision gives team members an overall sense of the purpose, so they see themselves as building a cathedral instead of laying stones. The leader's first task is to prayerfully craft a **vision statement** that encapsulates his or her vision for the ministry or assignment to which he or she has stewardship over. A vision statement is a written outline or description of the mental picture one possesses detailing one's future desire. The vision statement should provide answers to the ensuing questions:

✓ *What is the ultimate impact I desire to have on my local community, the church in general, and the world?*

✓ *In what way will the members of my ministry interact with people within the actual marketplace?*

✓ *What will the culture of my ministry look like, and how will that be demonstrated in the believers' lives?*

The leader's vision is pivotal to the growth of the institution and is necessary for the inspiration of the team. People will submit to and follow a leader who has a clear objective in mind even if he/she lacks the resources necessary to accomplish the goal and is unclear as to how to pursue it. Vision is what keeps people moving.

Where there is no vision, the people perish.

(Proverbs 29:18 KJV)

Vision is borne out of divine communication and therefore is a synopsis of God's intent. Where vision is lacking, the church, team, or group will lack restraint. Vision is not limited to the mental faculty of the leader but God's desire. A well thought out vision is necessary to inspire others to follow.

And you should imitate me, just as I imitate Christ.

(1 Corinthians 11:1)

QUALITIES OF A GOOD LEADER

The Impact of Passion on Leadership

"To succeed you have to believe in something with such passion that it becomes a reality."

-Anita Roddick

Previously we examined the impact of vision on leadership, now we will look keenly at passion.

What is Passion?

Passion is a solid or intense feeling of love, desire, and enthusiasm toward something. The leader must be passionate about his/her role and the vision itself if he/she is to successfully attract the best minds to his/her team and stir the interest of the members already serving his/her team (active members). The leader's passion will aid in motivating his/her team members to excel and serve selflessly and fervently. Sometimes, a team's disinterest is borne out of the lack of passion exhibited by the leader.

Dr. Myles Munroe posits "passion is contagious, and a leader is most effective when he/she is passionate about the team, organisation, and the work thereof." He further states, "passion is a characteristic that cannot be faked but must be genuine and portrayed."

 **Passion eliminates laziness and encourages industry**

Never be lazy but work hard and serve the Lord enthusiastically. ***-Romans 12:11***

Passion invites the support, commitment, and loyalty of others. When leaders are sincerely enthusiastic and passionate, it becomes contagious and spreads among the team quickly, inspiring onlookers.

How passionate are you about your ministry?

Passion will allow the leader to serve without considering the personal cost to fulfil the vision. It will propel the leader to serve even in the absence of financial reward or kindness. Therefore, to be passionate is to be intrinsically motivated. Pasion is the inner drive that empowers the leader to persevere persistently despite the presence of adversity or discomfort. The intrinsically motivated leader knows that **giving up is not an option**.

QUALITIES OF A GOOD LEADER
The Impact of Integrity on Leadership

"The greatness of a man is not in how much wealth he acquires, but in his integrity and his ability to affect those around him positively."

-Bob Marley

Earlier we discussed vision and passion and how it affects leadership, now we will examine **Integrity** and its impact on leadership.

What is Integrity?

Integrity is the quality of life characterised by Christlike principles and practices.

In everything, set them an example by doing what is good. In your teaching, show integrity and seriousness.

(Titus 2:7)

This is a lifestyle evidenced by the fruit of the Spirit as set out Galatians 5: 22b-23a: *...love, joy, peace, patience, kindness, goodness, faithfulness, gentleness, and self-control.*

A leader who is influenced by the Holy Spirit will be:

- **Honest**

The leader should be fair in his/her interaction when dealing with others. Honesty is the quality of being free from deceit, truthful, and sincere. *"Great leaders are not defined by the absence of weakness, but rather by the presence of clear strengths."* -John Zenger

- **Respectful**

This is the ability to show consideration, regard and honour to individuals, their opinions, and properties. To be respectful is to treat others with dignity. *Love each other with genuine affection and take delight in honoring each other.* **(Romans 12:10)**

The Bible encourages us to show respect even to those deemed unworthy. Peter, the day's leader, urged Christians to respect them though the Roman government persecuted them. We don't have to agree with you to respect you. Peter urges believers to *"show proper respect to everyone, love the family of believers, fear God, honour the emperor (1 Peter 2:17).* Respect is an expectation given to all regardless of the past, present, or future circumstances.

- **Trustworthy**

This is the degree to which one is dependable. A trustworthy leader will follow through on pledges and promises. He/she does not strive to impress through mere pretense but is consistent in his/her practices. A trustworthy leader is a great example of the quality expects from his/her team, and where he/she fails to meet the expectation, he/she will apologise profusely. A worthy leader is honest, transparent, confident, and predictable. *"No virtue is more universally accepted as a test of good character than trustworthiness."*- <u>Harry Emerson Fosdick</u>

- **Helpful**

Leadership entails giving help and support to all in need. He/she is always ready to help his/her team members. Leaders don't only cheer from the stance; they get involved. The willingness to come to the aid of others is a pertinent expectation of every leader. People desire to know that they can rely on the leader to provide quality assistance. Ideally, the leader should possess the skills, expertise, and knowledge. Where he/she is unable to provide the requite support, he/she should know where to source help. A real leader does not wait for things to go wrong; he/she intervenes wisely to support. The helpful leader does not micromanage; he/she observes and wisely intervenes. An effective leader creates a culture where helping is celebrated through example. This will likely enhance productivity and attract reciprocity. *"In helping others, we shall help ourselves, for whatever good we give out completes the circle and comes back to us."*- <u>Flora Edwards</u>

- **Good Communication Skills**

People are relational beings who function best when there is good communication, both written and oral. Communication is not limited to the ability to convey instructions but also entails the exchange of emotions. Therefore, Good communication is essential for creating a healthy working environment conducive to goal realisation. Thus, the leader must strive to develop and demonstrate strong communication skills such as:

- *Conveying information in a simple, concise, and unambiguous manner.*

- *The ability to utilise interpersonal skills, namely verbal and nonverbal communicators.*
- *The employment of aids to communicate inclusive of technology.*

The leader should create an environment where instructions are effectively communicated and understood. There should be frequent monitoring and following up to ensure messages are delivered effectively. The leader should be approachable and ready to provide additional support when required. John C. Maxwell posits, "leaders must be close enough to relate to others, but far enough ahead to motivate them." The work setting should be characterised as one in which information is transferred to produce understanding among the team members, enabling greater productivity and efficiency.

- **Celebration and Appreciation**

Observingly, one of the most notable elements of an underperforming team or organisation is one in which people feel unappreciated. No matter how well people are compensated, there is a strong desire to feel appreciated. People work selflessly, tirelessly and serve genuinely in churches, organisations, and teams where they are celebrated. Chad Brooks, in a 2013 Business article, posits that "A study conducted by an online career website known as Glassdoor revealed that more than 80 percent of employees confirmed that they are motivated to work harder when their boss shows appreciation for their work, compared to less than 40 percent who are inspired to work harder when their boss is demanding or because they fear losing their job." Celebration and appreciation are not always in the form of gifts and yearly events. People can get more money and still feel worthless. Therefore, a thorough distinction must be made between recognition and appreciation.

Recognition is acknowledging what people do. For example, "James is early for all his meetings; John made a great intro video for the church". However, appreciation is about acknowledging the value of people. People are the most valuable asset in every church, group, and team, which must be communicated at every opportunity through empathy and genuine compassion. *"As we look ahead into the next century, leaders will be those who empower others."* - <u>Bill Gates</u>

Leadership has more to do with how you treat people than it has to with your knowledge. Teddy Roosevelt opines, "People don't care how much you know until they know how much you care." Appreciation should not be reserved for special occasions but should be shown frequently, proactively, and meaningfully. In his work "Maslow Hierarchy of Needs," Abraham Maslow cited the need to feel love, belonging, and connectedness as essential for people.

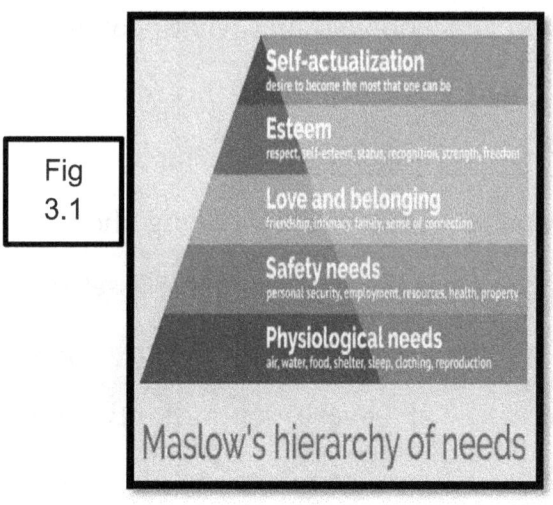

Fig 3.1

Whereas recognition is critical in showing appreciation is more about honouring people by fostering an atmosphere of acceptance, love, and connectivity. Influential leaders understand the value of demonstrating ongoing and sincere gratitude to the people he/she serves. *"The first responsibility of a leader is to define reality. The last is to say thank you. In between, the leader is a servant."*- Max DePree

Be an Ensample

The leader should be the precise sample (epitomy) of the qualities he/she expects from the members of his/her team. Therefore, the leader must invest in exemplifying the interpersonal, professional, and technological skills needed to ensure productivity. Brian Tracy encourages leaders to "become the kind of leader that people would follow voluntarily, even if you had no title or position." In addition, the leader must exhibit the courage to believe in the vision and pursue it selflessly. John Maxwell posits "a great leader's courage to fulfill his vision comes from passion, not position." People will serve a leader whose pursuit of the goal is inspired by his/her drive to honour God and fulfil the intended mission with excellence.

- **Be practical**

A practical leader is one who is:

✓ *Realistic:* He/she focuses on the essentials of all situations, whether favourable or not. A realistic leader constantly adjusts his/her plans to meet the current situation's demands to ensure the successful attainment of the goal. A realistic leader employs new strategies, modifies behaviour, and participates in formal and informal research to bolster success. Realistic leaders avoid the pitfalls of what things could be but instead focus on what is. Michael Jordan explains, "some people want it to happen, some wish it would happen, others make it happen."

✓ *Determined:* This leader sets clear goals and relentlessly pursues them. There is no space for wavering and or hesitation. When challenged, the determined leader reverts to the plan for a reminder, adapts to the circumstance, chooses a practical path, and passionately pursues the objective. For example, David was determined to stop Israel's misery, so much so that he offered to fight an experienced warrior. Though he did not readily have the support of his fellow countryman, he made this decision based on his faith in God and not his abilities.

David replied to the Philistine, "You come to me with sword, spear, and javelin, but I come to you in the name of the Lord of Heaven's Armies - the God of the armies of Israel, whom you have defied.

(1 Samuel 17:45)

✓ *Risk taking:* A common characteristic of the practical leader is risk-taking. He/she will often have to make a conscious decision based on the situation. Such decisions require an act of faith based on the leader's relationship with his God and his/her confidence in the ability and will of God. He/she must be decisive and willing to accept responsibility for any likely misfortune. Teammates are usually willing to take risks if they perceive the leader as trustworthy, practical, and realistic. For example, although outnumbered, the soldiers were ready to accompany Gideon to battle.

✓ *Intrinsically Motivated:* The practical leader does not rely on the praise, applause, or recognition of others; neither does he/she depend on others to approve or disapprove of the directive from the Lord. Instead, he/she is driven by love for the work of the Lord and the desire to honour Him. While there is wisdom in conversing and sharing with others what God is saying, a discussion in this manner is not for approval but for support, advice, and guidance to fulfill God's directives. God is the ultimate leader; therefore, His instructions do not require man's approval or validation.

- *Prioritisation:* Practical leaders are action-oriented and, as such, will need to prioritise to complete the mission at hand successfully. Doing several projects does not make one successful; learning to prioritise will. That is arranging the tasks in order of most important to least important. The pursuit of these steps in order of importance is what leads to ultimate success.

To prioritise, you must learn to be a practical thinker who, through conscious analysis, will determine the order through which tasks are to be completed. Eric Hoffer sums it up as "the leader must be practical, and a realist yet must talk the language of the visionary and the idealist."

THE HEART OF LEADERSHIP

"People who are truly strong lift others up. People who are truly powerful bring others together."
                                                    -Michelle Obama

Leadership is the art of guiding and influencing people to accomplish a goal in keeping with God's word and his divine will. The success of leadership is hinged on the ability of an individual to inspire others to complete a task, pursue a course of action, or serve within a mission while being faithful to God and His will. The leader should inspire others to follow even as he/she pursue God's instructions. Paul urged his followers to *imitate him, just as he imitates Christ (1 Corinthians 11:1).* It is God who establishes the principles of order, authority, and accountability. Paul opines *"the head of every man is Christ, the head of woman is man, and the head of Christ is God (1 Corinthians 1:2).*

Leadership requires:

- **An Awareness of Order**

The earthly leader must first submit to God with the desire to honour Him sincerely. He/she must recognise that the core of his/her purpose is to serve God willingly and earnestly influenced by an attitude is one of love and selflessness. Therefore, the leader must first become a participant who is an example of what he desires from those he/she leads because only then he is worthy of declaring "imitate me as I imitate Christ".

 **Order is at the epicentre of leadership.**

An Understanding of Authority

Leadership requires a clear distinction between the leader and the members of the team to allow for the transmission of clear directions and relaying of feedback. The leader is endowed with authority which is the legal and legitimate power to guide, manage, monitor, appraise, and provide meaningful feedback to members of his/her team. The leader must recognise God as the one with the ultimate authority as such must regularly seek clarity and guidance (prayer). Similarly, he/she must recognise that instructions come from God and therefore he should incline his ears on to God. As leader he/she should execute the task based on God's directive. God has the authority to reward members on the quality of service.

"Look, I am coming soon! My reward is with me, and I will give to each person. According to what they have done.
(Revelation 22:12)

Similarly, the leader has the authority to provide directives to the team, monitor their progress, and provide feedback accordingly. God has authorised the leader to reward his/her team accordingly.

- **Mutual Accountability**

The leader is expected to account for its activities, accept responsibility for them, and to disclose the results in a transparent manner." The apostle Paul sought to hold his mentee/associate pastor accountable by encouraging him in 1 Timothy 4:12: *Don't let anyone look down on you because you are young, but set an example for the believers in speech, in conduct, in love, in faith and in purity.*

Where order, authority, and accountability are missing there is chaos and confusion.

THE TASK OF LEADERSHIP

"A leader takes people where they want to go. A great leader takes people where they don't necessarily want to go, but ought to be."
- <u>Rosalynn Carter</u>

The Purposes of Leadership are:

- **Influencing Others**

The role of the leader is to inspire those he leads to excel holistically. *"Leadership is influence."* (John C. Maxwell). He/she must possess the capacity to significantly impact the character, conduct, and general way of life of the people he leads. People are social beings who learn through observational skills: hearing, feeling, and seeing. Given this reality, leaders will influence the team directly and indirectly, formally, and informally. This is exemplified in scripture when we examine the relationship between Elijah and Elisha. His mentor so influenced the younger prophet that he was willing to follow him despite several sources of discouragement. Leaders can have a lasting impact on the lives of those they lead.

- **Create Opportunities for Others**

An effective leader should generate opportunities for people to grow, develop, and be proficient. The leader must constantly look for new development opportunities and motivate the team to take on new challenges. A leader who only develops him/herself will quickly become obsolete and unattractive. The leader's investment in others raises his/her value and keeps him/her relevant. The team members will continuously admire their leader for helping them to advance.

- **Believe in the Team**

The most incredible empowerment and support one can give a person is relentless faith in his/her purpose and potential. The leader should frequently affirm each member of his/her team's worth and value. The leader should commend them when they do well and encourage them when the results are unappealing.

- **Put Others First**

The purpose driven leader considers the need of others above him or herself and as such willing to serve them selflessly. The growth and development of each team member are paramount to servant leadership.

- **Build Trust**

The leader should genuinely believe in the ability of his/her team members. It is trust that holds a team together. Working together enhances confidence and propels growth in the group. The leader must exhibit the right qualities to encourage the members to trust.

- **Extend Honour to Earn Honour**

Honour is given and not demanded. Honour offered, will be reciprocated; therefore, there is a direct correlation between honour given and honour received. To be earned, thus, the leader.

- **Invest in Others**

Leadership is deemed outstanding based on the leaders' impact on the people they lead. A manager directs while he/she is present. A leader guides even in absence. Leadership, therefore, requires the leader to pour wisdom and knowledge into his/her subordinates while instilling qualities that will enable them to function beyond the tenure or reign of the leader effectively. Leadership is about one leader investing in others to create a culture of greatness. Eric Greiger posits "leadership is a temporary assignment." Throughout the Bible ages, there have been several leaders, and they all reigned for only a period. So, it is within our local assemblies that even if you are the founder, you are merely human, strength will evade, death will prevail. At some point you will vacate your post whether by retirement, illnesses, or death. It is therefore incumbent for leaders to prepare others to succeed him/her. The continuation of a great vision relies heavily on the leader's investing in others. Leaders must view themselves as temporary steward serving God's mission. The mission remains intact, even as leaders change. The constancy of the task and the pending expiration of time allotted to lead is grounds to him/her to empower others to serve. Perhaps this is what informed Jethro's concern in Exodus 18:14, *"What are you really accomplishing here? Why are you trying to do all this alone while everyone stands around you from morning till evening?"*

PREPARING TO MORROW'S LEADERS

Jealousy is the result of one's lack of self-confidence, self-worth, and self-acceptance.

-Sasha Azevedo

The goal of leadership is never to produce a selfish and self-serving leader but rather a proactive one who uses every opportunity to prepare tomorrow's leader. Think of yourself as a member of an Olympic relay team whose role is to complete your leg of the journey and ready to hand it over to your successor. Like relay teams with coaches to prepare the next person to receive the baton, leaders must prepare persons to assume stewardship and excel at service. Like many leaders, Moses made several excuses for handling the assignment alone. Similarly, today, some leaders are cautious as relates to preparing successors for reasons such as:

- *fear that the individuals will somehow overthrow them.*
- *fear that the persons may split the church to start their own ministries.*
- *fear that the individuals will leave the ministry to enhance another.*
- *lack of trust for the people within the ministry.*
- *thinking that only him or her (the leader) can do an excellent job.*

These views are detrimental to the completion of God's mission. Leaders must constantly remind themselves that the mission belongs to God. Our frail bodies, coupled with our best effort, will not be able to fulfill God's mission. We must therefore excel at our assignments during our tenure. At the core of our service, we must prepare others to continue where our tenures end.

Who are you Investing in Today?

Jethro cautioned Moses: *"This is not good!" Moses' father-in-law exclaimed (Exodus 18:17).* He then encouraged him to divest and replicate his leadership qualities in others.

"You're going to wear yourself out—and the people, too. This job is too heavy a burden for you to handle all by yourself. Now listen to me, and let me give you a word of advice, and may God be with you. You should continue to be the people's representative before God, bringing their disputes to him. Teach them God's decrees and give them his instructions. Show them how to conduct their lives. But select from all the people some capable, honest men who fear God and hate bribes. Appoint them as leaders of groups of one thousand, one hundred, fifty, and ten. They should always be available to solve the people's common

disputes but have them bring the major cases to you. Let the leaders decide the smaller matters themselves. They will help you carry the load, making the task easier for you.

Joshua was the product of this investment made by Moses. Consequently, he was prepared to lead the people toward the objective, the promised land. After the death of Moses, the Lord's servant, the Lord spoke to Joshua, *"Moses my servant is dead. Therefore, the time has come for you to lead these people, the Israelites, across the Jordan River into the land I am giving them.* **(Joshua 1:1-2)**

Although Moses' leadership tenure ended, Joshua continued to serve the mission. Do not allow your church or ministry to struggle. You are not indispensable; invest in tomorrow's leader. Ralph Nader concurs that the function of leadership is to produce more leaders, not more followers.

CHOOSING THE MOST EFFECTIVE LEADERSHIP STYLE

"It's not about making the right choice. It's about making a choice and making it right."

- *J.R. Rim*

There is no finer example for Christian leadership than our Lord Jesus Christ. He called himself the good shepherd. (John 10:11). This scripture provides a perfect description of a Christian leader. Before we examine the styles of leadership let's examine the role of the leader. Regardless of your leadership style these are the functions of the Christian leader. He/she acts as a shepherd to those "sheep" in his care. Examining his/her role as sheep requires us to explore sheep and the shepherd with the first century.

An Examination of the Sheep

When Jesus referred to us as "sheep," He was not speaking in affectionate terms. Sheep rank among the dumbest animals in creation likely to go astray frequently evading the shepherd. A sheep easily becomes disoriented, confused, frightened, and incapable of finding its way back to the flock. They are unable to defend themselves against fierce predators, making it the most helpless of all creatures. Sheep are known to drown during times of torrential flooding even in sight of easily accessible higher ground. Be aware of all this, the good shepherd labelled us sheep, implying without a shepherd, we are helpless. People need effective leaders.

An Examination of the Shepherd

The shepherd has several roles regarding his sheep. He leads, feeds, nurtures, comforts, corrects, and protects. The shepherd leads by modeling godliness and righteousness in his own life and encouraging others to follow his example.

The shepherd is a feeder and a nourisher of the sheep. The ultimate "sheep food" is the Word of God. Just as the shepherd leads his flock to the lushest pasture so they can grow and flourish, the Christian leader nourishes his flock with the God's word producing strong, vibrant Christians.

The shepherd comforts the sheep, binding up their wounds and applying the balm of compassion and love. People in today's world suffer many injuries to their spirits. Therefore, they need compassionate leaders to bear their burdens, sympathise with them, exhibit patience, encourage them in the Word, and pray for them. This is the hallmark of good leadership.

Just as the shepherd used his crook to pull a wandering sheep back into the fold, the leader should correct and discipline those in his care when they go astray. Without rancor or an overbearing spirit, but with a "spirit of gentleness" (Galatians 6:1), those in leadership must correct according to scriptural principles. Correction or discipline is never a pleasant experience for either party, but the Christian leader who fails in this area is not exhibiting love for those in his care. "The LORD disciplines those he loves" (Proverbs 3:12), and the Christian leader must follow His example.

Finally, the shepherd protects his sheep. The predators of today are those trying to lure the sheep away with false doctrine, dismissing the Bible as quaint and old fashioned, insufficient, unclear, or unknowable. These lies are spread by those against whom Jesus warned us: "Watch out for false prophets. They come to you in sheep's clothing, but inwardly they are ferocious wolves" (Matthew 7:15). Leaders must protect his/her sheep from the false teachings of those who attempt to lead them astray.

Fulfilling these vital roles requires us to examine our strengths, uncovering our style of leadership. The more we know about ourselves the more likely we are lead God's flock. In the subsequent chapters we will explore four styles of leadership.

There are a variety of leadership styles both traditional and contemporary. Choosing the most effective for a situation will require one to first be aware of the varying styles of leadership. While there is no ideal leadership style that will match all circumstances, a thorough knowledge of the staples is necessary when discerning and deciding which to use in a particular scenario. A single scenario may require a leader to adopt a mixed approach therefore it is imperative to examine all. Leadership styles can be categorised as autocratic/authoritarian, democratic/participative, laissez-faire, delegate, transformational, transactional, charismatic, and supportive.

CHOOSING THE MOST EFFECTIVE LEADERSHIP STYLE

The Boss Regime (Autocratic/Authoritarian)

"A boss has the title; the leader has the people."

-Simon Sinek

In this chapter we will examine The Boss Regime (Autocratic/Authoritarian) Leadership Style

The Boss Regime (Autocratic/Authoritarian)

This leadership style is characterised by a person (leader) who controls all the decision making within a group, church, or organisation. The leader is the primary acceptable source of information and rarely accepts input, ideas, or suggestions from his/her team members. In such settings, members are dictated to and expected to conform to the rigid processes. Autocratic leadership is task driven; thus, the leader is more concerned about the objectives and outlook of the church, organisation, team, or group than the welfare of those he/she leads. Within an authoritarian environment, productivity is generally lower. Whenever goals are unsuccessful, members are more concerned about evading strict punishment. They work without passion as they typically feel like mere objects. Tension is sometimes high as people are often uncomfortable. They think of themselves as robots working to meet objectives on a checklist rather than people contributing to the livelihood of the entity. Within a 'Boss Regime' the leader often uses statements like:

- *I am the pastor/leader/director.*
- *I run things.*
- *Whatever I say goes.*
- *You will ...*
- *This is what I want you.*

These statements are generally spoken and reiterated with condescending tones highlighting the little value placed on the team members. Not only does the boss share little regard for people but also for the wisdom of God. In Luke 18, Jesus shares a parable of an unjust judge. Luke's account of the story described the judge as unjust, one who did not fear God or man. Although this parable is intended to teach persistence in prayer, one cannot ignore the main character's attitude in the analogy. His attitude is one of pride; as such, he would not listen to the needs of those he served. Leadership is about serving people, not only attaining goals. The judge was unwilling to engage with the woman before concluding his action. It was simply "his way or the highway."

The word judge, derived from the Greek word "κριτής" which means referee and umpire, opposes the very attitude he displayed. No leader should be wise in his/her own eyes. The authors of this book enjoy watching football despite supporting different teams. The on-field referee often controls the game, but this does prevent him/her from consulting his/her two linesmen/women or the virtual assistant referee before deciding. Consultation helps to achieve the right results and shows that we are interdependent. No man is an island. Likewise, in cricket, the umpire consults with his third umpire before deciding that a player is out or declaring a boundary. Our position determines perspectives; consultation helps us to gain insight into the bigger picture.

The judge showed no interest in discussing the matter with anyone in the text. Regardless of what anyone else knew, his word was final. Luke declared, "he did not fear God nor regard man." Decisions are the prerogative of leadership, but they must never be made selfishly without a willingness to analyse the circumstances carefully. The one with power must take care so as not to become corrupt.

People want to feel valued and belong. Where this is missing, discomfort will prevail.

The "boss regime":
- *Permits little or no input from members of the group, team, or church.*
- *Requires leaders to make all decisions disregarding the ideas, input of others.*
- *Makes provision for the leader to dictate work methods and processes.*
- *Creates an atmosphere where members feel they are not trusted with decisions or important tasks.*
- *Instills highly structured and extremely rigid environments.*
- *Discourages creative thinking and rejects news ideas.*
- *Develops rules to maintain control.*

CHOOSING THE MOST EFFECTIVE LEADERSHIP STYLE

The "Hands Off" Leader (Laissez faire)

"Great leaders are almost always great simplifiers, who can cut through argument, debate and doubt to offer a solution everybody can understand."

-Gen. Colin Powell

In this leadership style, the leader adopts a laid-back approach leaving the responsibility of decision making up to others within the group, team, church, or organisation. The leader usually relies upon members to use initiative, be creative, and implement strategies to fulfill goals. Owing to the unwavering confidence in the members' abilities, little to no guidance is provided. Instructions are blurred and left up to the initiative of each member. Communication is often ineffective and may lead to catastrophic outcomes.

Whereas some people would enjoy this leadership style, comfort is the enemy to progress. Sometimes a member will never know how much he/she can do without the "gentle push" of a leader. Clear instructions reduce chaos and confusion by providing the necessary guidance to attain productivity. While inclusion is essential for making meaningful decisions, too much freedom can lead to low productivity, confusion, decline in interpersonal relationships, and a general breakdown in values and social conduct. This type of leadership promotes a setting in which it is difficult to recognise who is in charge.

In Genesis, God made Adam's steward of the Garden of Eden.

The Lord God placed the man in the Garden of Eden to tend and watch over it. ***(Genesis 2:15)***

The Lord gave him precise instructions for his assignment as manager of the Garden. Adam seemingly adopted a "hands off" approach to leadership, allowing those under his leadership to make decisions without first consulting with him. The serpent, therefore, got Eve to sign off on a decision that should have been approved by Adam after careful consultation with the Chief Executive Officer of Eden, El Elohim.

The serpent was the shrewdest of all the wild animals the Lord God had made. One day he asked the woman, "Did God really say you must not eat the fruit from any of the trees in the garden?"

"Of course, we may eat fruit from the trees in the garden," the woman replied. "It's only the fruit from the tree in the middle of the garden that we are not allowed to eat. God said, 'You must not eat it or even touch it; if you do, you will die. You won't die!" the serpent replied to the woman. God knows that your eyes will be opened as soon as you eat it, and you will be like God, knowing both good and evil. The woman was convinced. She saw that the tree was beautiful, and its fruit looked delicious, and she wanted the wisdom it would give her. So, she took some of the fruit and ate it." **(Genesis 3:1-6)**

Adam's laid-back approach further led to him following the lead of the one task to follow (Eve), which subsequently led to both being terminated from the Garden of Eden. Some aspects of leadership may be delegated but not decision making.

Then she gave some to her husband, who was with her, and he ate it, too. **(Genesis 3:7)**

The CEO's (God) obvious disapproval of Adam's assignment handling led to severe consequences for the first family. Leaders must be firm and decisive, ready to hold people accountable. Then he said to the woman, *"I will sharpen the pain of your pregnancy, and in pain you will give birth. And you will desire to control your husband, but he will rule over you. And to the man he said, "Since you listened to your wife and ate from the tree whose fruit, I commanded you not to eat, the ground is cursed because of you. All your life you will struggle to scratch a living from it. It will grow thorns and thistles for you, though you will eat its grains. By the sweat of your brow will you have food to eat until you return to the ground from which you were made."*

(Genesis 3: 16-19)

You can still love, and respect people yet hold people accountable for the wrong done. Although He still loved Adam, he showed him that mediocrity was unacceptable. Holding you accountable does not make you an enemy.

CHOOSING THE MOST EFFECTIVE LEADERSHIP STYLE

The Irresponsible Leader

"The mediocre teacher tells. The good teacher explains. The superior teacher demonstrates. The great teacher inspires."

-William Arthur Ward

This is an approach to leadership in which the leader willfully defies order, precepts, and is reluctant to submit to an accountable mentor, or oversight body. The leader is often rigid and uses various means to manipulate those he leads, instilling fear and demanding loyalty from him/her. Anyone who fails to submit to such ordinances is perceived and treated as an outcast. The unaccountable leader makes decisions and declarations void of proper research, evaluation, reflection, or intercession. He/she is willing to satisfy his/her ego at any cost, even if it means putting the lives and livelihood of those to whom he/she leads. This leader is more concerned about how he/she is perceived than making objective and responsible decisions. This leader disregards accountability and often perceives him/herself to be the chief among the righteous. While followers are loyal, they lack the willpower to think, assess, and offer an amicable opinion and usually fear disrespect and isolation, so they remain quiet.

This leader will never take responsibility for his/her action; rather, he/she will attempt to justify. During the battle, Saul regarded protocol and offered sacrifice to the Lord. Meanwhile, Saul stayed at Gilgal, and his men were afraid.

Saul waited there seven days for Samuel, as Samuel had instructed him earlier, but Samuel still didn't come. Saul realised that his troops were rapidly slipping away. So, he demanded, "Bring me the burnt offering and the peace offerings!" And Saul sacrificed the burnt offering himself.

(1 Samuel 13:7-9)

In the press of the immediate crisis, Saul disregarded the prophet's instruction for what he thought was more feasible. Your perception of the situation should not be the basis for disobeying procedures, laws, or policies. Instead, a responsible should consult with superior leaders, stakeholders, and the eternal God. Solid decisions are the product of consultation, both earthly and Godly.

 **Do not function as an individualist. You are a part of a greater body.**

Saul aptness to operate as an individualist earned him the rebuke of the prophet.

"How foolish!" Samuel exclaimed. "You have not kept the command the Lord your God gave you. Had you kept it, the Lord would have established your kingdom over Israel forever. But now your kingdom must end, for the Lord has sought out a man after his own heart. The Lord has already appointed him to be the leader of his people, because you have not kept the Lord's command."

(1 Samuels 13:13-14)

CHOOSING THE MOST EFFECTIVE LEADERSHIP STYLE

The "No Guts" Leadership Style

"The greatest leader is not necessarily the one who does the greatest things. He is the one that gets the people to do the greatest things."

-President Ronald Reagan

The leader possessing this leadership style is perceived as weak, lacking the courage to make difficult decisions. He/she is more concerned about the feelings of others than good governance. This leader is often taken for granted by those he leads, resulting in missed deadlines, delays, and disrespect. The working atmosphere is most of the time uncomfortable, and weaker members are often preyed on by predators. Members continually seek solace outside of the group. Violators are protected and often get away with misdemeanour as the leader cannot hold them accountable.

In the book Samuel, we meet a high priest called Eli whose sons, also priests, were allowed to participate in varying unscrupulous acts while serving as a priest. The Bible describes the Hophni and Phineas as corrupt.

Now the sons of Eli were scoundrels who had no respect for the Lord or for their duties as priests. Whenever anyone offered a sacrifice, Eli's sons would send over a servant with a three-pronged fork. While the meat of the sacrificed animal was still boiling, the servant would stick the fork into the pot and demand that whatever it brought up be given to Eli's sons... **(1 Samuels 2: 12-17)**

The Bible refers to them as the sons of Belial (the pagan idol), meaning worthless and wicked men. They earned the description from their irregular practices, including violence, threats, coercion, and intimidation of those who came to offer sacrifice. The sons often engaged in sexually immoral acts with the women who assembled for worship.

Now Eli was very old, but he was aware of what his sons were doing to the people of Israel. He knew, for instance, that his sons were seducing the young women who assisted at the entrance of the Tabernacle. **(1 Samuels 2: 22)**

The High Priest lacked the firmness to restrain his sons accountable for their actions, which may have encouraged them to continue participating in the illicit acts.

Eli said to them, "I have been hearing reports from all the people about the wicked things you are doing. Why do you keep sinning? You must stop, my sons! The reports I hear among the Lord's people are not good. If someone sins against another person, God can mediate for the guilty party. But if someone sins against the Lord, who can intercede?" But Eli's sons wouldn't listen to their father, for the Lord was already planning to put them to death.

(1 Samuel 2:22-24)

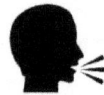 **Sin magnifies where there is no accountability.**

Transgression is most prevalent when the leader lacks the willpower to encourage righteous living and inspire submission to the ordinances of the LORD.

CHOOSING THE MOST EFFECTIVE LEADERSHIP STYLE

The "Honour at All Cost" Leadership Style

"A leader is one who sees more than others see, who sees farther than others see and who sees before others see."
— *Leroy Eimes*

In this approach to leadership, the leader is committed to bestowing honour to his/her superior officer, God, even if it costs him/her some allies, resources, and support. This individual is faithful to God's mission and will embrace the pain of ascribing worship to God. While aiming to develop good interpersonal relationships, this leader is not focused on being everyone's friend; instead, he/she desires to please God. This leader is concerned about getting the team to submit to God's will and live totally on God. The "honour at all costs" leader perceives him/herself merely as God's representative to the people; as such, he/she is cognisant that the people belong to God. Knowing this, the leader must focus on leading the people as God orders.

Honour in the Bible means to "esteem, value, or show great respect." To honour someone is to value him highly, showing tremendous respect. This leader is committed to honour God and His Son, Jesus Christ, by acknowledging that strength and wisdom come from God. He/she frequently confesses his/her weaknesses and relies on Him for directives. His/her limitation invites him/her to trust God. He/she refuses to dishonour God even for a season. He/she lives giving honour and obeisance to God through our humble adoration and obedience.

CHOOSING THE MOST EFFECTIVE LEADERSHIP STYLE

The Game Changer Leadership Style "Jesus".

"If your actions inspire others to dream more, learn more, do more and become more, you are a leader."

-President John Adams

This leadership style is one in which the leader examines the current vision to identify shortcomings and works collectively with their team to generate transformation through inspiration and the willingness to develop new and innovative strategies while carefully considering historical data, procedures, and processes. The game changer does not merely follow a pattern; this leader is willing to evaluate, adapt, recommend, and implement the change necessary to ensure the successful completion of the project, task, or mission. The game changer constantly engages in lifelong learning with the desire to provide high-quality leadership to the team/church/group and ensure the realisation of all short-term goals in pursuit of the long-term vision. The game changer is a creative thinker who is always willing to take calculated risks informed by critical thinking, continuous consultation, and consistent prayer. This type of leadership is highly interactive. Therefore, the leader is responsible for inspiring, motivating, and directing the team members toward the intended goal while crediting their input. This leader inspires team members to accomplish tasks effectively without micromanagement or coercion. All team members know the goals and are motivated to serve relentlessly, selflessly, and passionately. This leadership style creates a platform for new leaders to evolve through constant coaching, mentorship, and education. Emerging leaders can generate and implement ideas with robust support from more mature leaders. New leaders are seen as partners (shareholders) working to enhance and expand the vision, not competitors trying to deter success or destabilise the team's progress. Game changers are always looking for potential leaders to empower rather than exploit. This leadership style is observed in St Matthew 4:19, in which Jesus recognised the potential of the two brothers, Simon and Andrew, to serve, support, and lead people to realise Jesus' vision.

Jesus called out to them, "Come, follow me, and I will show you how to fish for people!" **(Matthew 4:19)**

In their own eyes, they were merely fishermen lacking the expertise to be successful in ministry. Simon and Andrew were not known to be articulate, possessing the ability to persuade an audience to follow Christ, a valuable skill for ministry. But Jesus, the game changer, saw international evangelists and apostles, men with great potential, that, if taught, could take the message of hope to various parts of the earth (Acts 1:8). The game changer can recognise the untapped potential in the people he serves. This type of leader continuously looks for people to empower and is responsible for unearthing overlooked abilities and redirecting talents and skills to fulfill purpose through coaching, mentorship, counselling, teaching, modelling, demonstration, and training. Throughout Jesus' ministry, He taught, enlightened, empowered, and encouraged people to which He administered over.

One day as he saw the crowds gathering, Jesus went up on the mountainside and sat down. His disciples gathered and he began to teach them. **(Matthew 5:1-2)**

Within this leadership style, leaders act decisively in addressing matters of morality. Jesus' boldly defended the values of the institution He represented and the vision He was sent to serve. You cannot sit by in silence when people fail in their service; you must point out the error, clarify expectations, provide honest feedback, and guide individuals through a process of improvement. The temple was a place set apart for God and was supposed to serve the purpose of prayer. In St. John 2: 14-16, Jesus, being perturbed by the unethical acts of the temple leaders, deliberately tried to address the matter.

In the Temple area he saw merchants selling cattle, sheep, and doves for sacrifices; he also saw dealers at tables exchanging foreign money. Jesus made a whip from some ropes and chased them all out of the Temple. He drove out the sheep and cattle, scattered the money changers' coins over the floor, and turned over their tables. Then, going over to the people who sold doves, he told them, "Get these things out of here. Stop turning my Father's house into a marketplace!"

Game changers must pay attention to irregularities and take steps to resolve these matters urgently. The leader must conduct a proper assessment to balance justice and mercy when dealing with undesired interpersonal conduct. Disagreements are normal and are sometimes necessary for the growth of the group, members, church, and organisation. Therefore, the game changer must carefully analyse and assess all scenarios case-by-case before deciding. The leader must always seek to recognise the motive and apply compassion and mercy when handling disputes. In St John 8:4-10, the writer shares an account in which Jesus was called upon to resolve an issue with an adulterous woman and her accusers.

"Teacher," they said to Jesus, "this woman was caught in the act of adultery. The Law of Moses says to stone her. What do you say?" They were trying to trap him into saying something they could use against him, but Jesus stooped down and wrote in the dust with his finger. They kept demanding an answer, so he stood up again and said,

"All right, but let the one who has never sinned throw the first stone!" Then he stooped down again and wrote in the dust. When the accusers heard this, they slipped away one by one, beginning with the oldest, until only Jesus was left in the middle of the crowd with the woman. Then Jesus stood up again and said to the woman, "Where are your accusers? Didn't even one of them condemn you?"

The fundamental goal of the game changer is to produce disciples and not fans. That is, people whose lifestyles are informed by the scriptures regarding God as their only hero.

I appointed you to go and produce lasting fruit, so that the Father will give you whatever you ask for, using my name.
(John 15:16b)

The game changer is a strong advocate for succession planning recognising that for the ministry to be sustainable, there needs to be constant recruitment, training, and deployment of trained personnel to fulfill the assignment. The recruits must have as their number one criterion loyalty to the vision and a willingness to serve. 2 Timothy 2:2 The vision must be embraced and owned by those being developed who will be responsible for empowering the next set of leaders. One of the unique skill sets of the game changer is the ability to identify and empower the leader.

DEVELOP AN ACTION PLAN

"There are no secrets to success. It is the result of preparation, hard work, and learning from failure."
-Colin Powell

Administration requires detail and purposeful planning as one of the leader's fundamental roles is developing a workable plan to guide the members, groups, or church to the intended goal. This type of plan is called an action plan. An action plan is a list of activities, tasks, or objectives to be completed to fulfill a mission. In essence, it is a course of action to be undertaken to accomplish a goal. This plan must be developed while considering the overall vision of the group, team, church, or organisation. In the case of the church, the central vision is that all men would come to repentance through the gospel of Jesus Christ. The vision describes the intended future of the group, team, church, or organisation. The future of the church is the ultimate fellowship with God throughout eternity. All team, group, church, or organisation members live with this Hope in mind. And even when he reached the land God promised him, he lived there by faith—for he was like a foreigner, living in tents. And so did Isaac and Jacob, who inherited the same promise.

Abraham was confidently looking forward to a city with eternal foundations, a city designed and built by God.

(Hebrews 11:10)

Jesus, during His time on earth, based His message on this vision that redeemed men would reside together in harmony with God as was intended from the beginning of creation. From then on Jesus began to preach, *"Repent of your sins and turn to God, for the Kingdom of Heaven is near.* **(Matthew 4:17)**

The vision later gives rise to the mission. The mission is a critical assignment given to the members of a team, group, church, or organisation to pursue until it achieves the intended goal. It outlines how the members will accomplish each task in the vision. Our great leader Jesus defines the mission of His church, not the pastor or other earthly prelates.

Therefore, go and make disciples of all the nations, baptizing them in the name of the Father and the Son and the Holy Spirit. Teach these new disciples to obey all the commands I have given you. And be sure of this: I am with you always, even to the end of the age."

(Matthew 28:19-20)

The leader must therefore generate an action plan with the following aims:

- *Leading the team, group, members, and church toward God's ultimate vision.*
- *Making disciples as set out in the great commission.*

The leader is responsible for evaluating current activities and determining if they align with God's mission for His church. Some questions to ask are:

- *Will this activity lead to the redemption of men?*
- *Will this activity culminate with the salvation of men?*
- *Will this activity provide a framework for improving, empowering, and deploying other disciples?*
- *Does this activity edify the believer?*
- *Does it provide an opportunity for the birth of new believers?*

If the answer to any of the above-stated questions is "no," the activity may require some adjustment. All action plans must begin and end with Christ's vision and mission in mind, and all objectives must lead to an outcome that is in keeping with God's vision and mission for His church.

STEPS TO DEVELOPING AN EFFECTIVE ACTION PLAN

"The task of leadership is not to put greatness into humanity, but to elicit it, for the greatness is already there." —*John Buchan*

How to Develop an Effective Action Plan?

The leader can develop an actionable plan by:

1. **Defining the problem.** The definition of the problem sets out the reason for pursuing an event such as a conference, workshop, crusade, or forum. In defining the problem, ask yourself:
   - *What is happening that needs to be corrected?*
   - *What is going on well that may require this program or intervention?*

Knowledge of God's vision and mission will help the leader recognise problems, which are pivotal for constructing an action plan.

2. **Carefully outline the goal or objective.** Having identified the problem that is the reason for the intervention, the leader must then proceed in formulating the objective for the activity. Here are some questions to ask here:
   - *What do I hope to achieve?*
   - *What changes will I see in the end?*

   Your goals or objectives should be SMART.
   - S- Specific
   - M- Measurable
   - A- Attainable
   - R- Realistic/Reliable
   - T- Time

3. **Consult with God and fellow stakeholders.** Prayer must play a crucial role in the development of any plan. God is the originator of the vision. He directs the ultimate assignment, so the leader needs to discuss the matter with Him to gain insight, clarity, understanding, additional directives, and approval.

If you need wisdom, ask our generous God, and he will give it to you. He will not rebuke you for asking.

(James 1:5)

Leadership does not always mean generating new ideas; sometimes, it is working to improve a project previously undertaken by someone else. Understanding that others have worked on and are currently working on resolving the issue you are passionate about is helpful. As with Science and Technology, there is no need to reinvent the wheel but rather to develop the work that others have started. People are experts in their own right; learn as much as possible from them. Even those who have failed before can teach you all you need to avoid failure. Being mindful of this, the leader must frequently consult to gain insight and wisdom and learn from the experience of others.

Fools think their own way is right, but the wise listen to others. **(Proverbs 12:15)**

4. **Implement the most effective plan.** Now that you have carefully devised the plan, the leader must activate this plan in collaboration with the team, group, members, church, or organisation. The execution of the plan must be done in keeping with God's will to maximise success. Follow God's recipe to acquire greatness; any deviation may lead to disappointment.

Commit your actions to the Lord, and your plans will succeed. **(Proverbs 16: 3)**

5. **Frequent Monitoring and evaluation of the plan.** The successful completion of the assignment requires the leader to provide ongoing support through ongoing supervision; this means supervising everyone in completing the part of the project assigned repeatedly and continuously. Such intentional support tends to stimulate the interests of the members tasked to work on the assignment while providing meaningful guidance, support, and feedback to improve productivity and relationships. Effective feedback must be timely, regular, clear, and precise, allowing time for questions and answers. The goal of feedback is to improve the quality of work and ultimately ensure the successful completion of the project. Regular evaluation is necessary to discern weaknesses and create a

solution through supervisory support quickly. Assessment may be formal or informal but must be done repetitively and incrementally. At the end of the project, a final evaluation is needed to determine what criteria were achieved, recognise those aspects that went well and those requiring improvements. The report from this evaluation should be considered when developing and executing future plans.

Even worthwhile endeavors need evaluation to determine if they have become distractions from the best goals. - Quentin L. Cook

Therefore, there is a need for the group led by the leader to constantly analyse programs, assignments, processes, and procedures to determine their effectiveness in fulfilling Christ's mission and His vision for His people. You can pursue several activities and still fail to create an impact. Mark shares an account of Jesus cursing a fig tree because it had leaves but no fruit. It is better to analyse the project and determine what needs improvement than to proceed on a path of failure. In the story of Jesus and the fig tree, He cursed it because it had leaves and no figs. The tree was cursed for its pretense of leaves, not for its lack of fruit. Symbolically the tree was God's people, and their mission was to produce fruit. The fig tree's fruit generally appears before the leaves, and because the fruit is green, it blends in with the leaves right up until it is almost ripe. Therefore, when Jesus and His disciples saw from a distance that the tree had leaves, they immediately insinuated it had fruit on it even though it was earlier in the season. From a distance, a project can appear progressive; likewise, the team seems to excel. Don't just appear industrious, be industrious. Evaluate regularly to avoid ultimate failure.

Jesus' hunger in the story represents His passion for seeing His people excel, people who don't only present a good look externally but those who bear the fruit of the Father. The leader must likewise passionately evaluate to guarantee actual progress.

Having conducted a detailed and meaningful assessment, the leader should define the problem, create purposeful goals, seek the guidance of God and others with expertise, skills, and wisdom, implement the most suitable plan, and constantly monitor and assess the implementation of the program.

PLAN WITH AN OUTCOME IN MIND

"Create a definite plan for carrying out your desire and begin at once, whether you are ready or not, to put this plan into action."

- Napoleon Hill

At an educator workshop, the presenter explained, "Always plan with an outcome in mind as by doing so, you will be guided by what is to be and not what is." Too often, leaders become discouraged because the desired outcome does not readily happen. Sometimes the only motivation one has is the dream of what can be, hence make a big, yet realistic plan and use it to guide your every step. When contractors begin constructing a building, they start with the plan ("blueprint"). Before commencing the project, the contractor studies the building plan to understand the expectation. Constant reference is made to this plan during the execution of the project to ensure that the contractor delivers the correct product. The plan allows for redirection; it keeps the team on track. The plan is an effective motivator; it informs milestones and timeframes. The blueprint (building plan) is used to evaluate the project to determine if the intended goal was accomplished at the end of construction. The contractor (construction leader) is constantly guided by the blueprint (plan).

 A good plan guides progressively and culminates with a successful ending.

This ending of the plan must always be the light that guides the leader through the darkness. It is what the leader turns to in moments of frustration, uncertainty, and adversity. The plan must therefore be comprehensive, the inspiration for the vision. Before the leader develops a plan, ask:

- *Why am I engaging in this activity/project?*
- *What do I hope to achieve?*
- *Who will be impacted by this project?*
- *Is this plan realistic/ feasible?*

In addition to prayer and consultation among the team, the leader should think critically about the outcome of this project, as the perceived outcome will serve as the guide to the desired end. The plan must be realistic and practical to inspire others to share. Determining the practicality of a plan and its outcome requires meticulous research. The leader must have a mental concept of the outcome of the project to be undertaken. Developing a mental idea of the goal will also help one foresee the challenges ahead and devise effective strategies to navigate those difficult moments. The presence of obstacles does not always mean detour or cancellation;

sometimes, challenges mean you need to engage in more research and preparation. Having analysed the outcome, the leader should make a written description or outline of the plan highlighting its outcome. From the description, the leader should generate a list of success criteria. The success criteria are the standard by which the project outcome will be deemed successful. For example, the outcome of the course "Critical Keys for Marketplace Evangelism" is to assist students in understanding evangelism within the marketplace. This understanding will equip and empower scholars to use the Gospel as a tool for transformation within the marketplace globally.

The success criteria:
- *Students will develop an understanding of evangelism within the marketplace.*
- *Students will be able to identify and develop an understanding of the marketplace.*

- *Students will be equipped and empowered to share the gospel in the marketplace.*

This evangelistic course was developed with the product in mind: the desire to create and empower disciples to share the Gospel of Christ with the world. At the end of pursuing the course, the student can use the success criteria to evaluate each objective stated to determine if it was successful. Therefore, the success criteria are vital for determining the project's overall success and are useful for revision and improvement.

Throughout the planning and execution of this course, the planners have consistently referred to the success criteria to make decisions, such as lessons to be taught, type of assessment, and learning strategies.

Therefore, the successful completion is not by mere coincidence, but the purposeful and discipline application as guided by the success criteria. So, it is with developing your plan as the leader, and it should be planned with the mental conceptualisation of the outcome at the forefront of your mind and used to guide the general execution.

MOBILISATING THE TEAM

My own definition of leadership is this: The capacity and the will to rally men and women to a common purpose and the character which inspires confidence.
-General Montgomery

Michael Jordan posits that "talent wins games, but teamwork and intelligence win competitions." While this might be true to an extent, choosing and assigning your team is critical to leadership. Accomplishing a task may be possible single-handedly; nonetheless, the assistance of a team may make the process easier and more efficient. For example, one person can move a bed; however, when the same task is done as a team, the result will likely be accomplished more quickly and effectively. Not only does the team bring physical help but their intellectual property which may play a critical role in how the task is approached, executed, and fulfilled. Solomon posits: *"two people are better off than one, for they can help each other succeed. If one person falls, the other can reach out and help. But someone who falls alone is in real trouble."* **(Ecclesiastes 4:9-10)**

In acknowledging the pertinence of a team approach, the wise man posits that when two work with each other, they can accomplish more than each one would do. They provided a sense of security and safety as they relied on each other to complete a given assignment, thus boosting productivity, support, and help.

A person standing alone can be attacked and defeated, but two can stand back-to-back and conquer.

(Ecclesiastes 4:12a)

Solomon concludes his argument by suggesting that the unity of the three cords is less likely to be broken than the single cord.

Three are even better, for a triple-braided cord is not easily broken. ***(Ecclesiastes 4:12b)***

The three-fold in the text may be perceived as the leader, his team, and God, the giver of all assignments. The three are robust, sturdy, and incapable of being halted by any opposition.

The best team is needed to achieve the mandate. Christ demonstrated appreciation for teamwork when he physically selected a team to aid with the assignment. Though He was God and could accomplish all things by Himself perfectly, he sought help. Seeking assistance does not equate to personal weakness or incompetence. Missions are best completed in the company of others who share your interests. If the eternal God who made all things saw the need for a team, what justification do we have to work as lone soldiers? Matthew explains that Jesus selected a team with the goal of preparing Him to fulfil His vision.

"One day as Jesus was walking along the shore of the Sea of Galilee, he saw two brothers—Simon, also called Peter, and Andrew—throwing a net into the water, for they fished for a living. Jesus called out to them, "Come, follow me, and I will show you how to fish for people!" And they left their nets at once and followed him.

(Matthew 4:18-20)

Although Christ has no personal limitation, the time set to accomplish His goal of creating a way to restore all man to himself had a timeframe. His time on earth as a mere human was restricted. Christ being aware of His limited time within the earth domain, knew that the continuity of the vision depends primarily on Him recruiting, training, empowering, and mobilising the best team. Like Christ, we are temporary stewards who must prepare a team to expand the vision successfully.

How to Choose your Team?

Groups, churches, and teams are unique in culture, resources, and approaches. We will attempt give a formula as no particular formula will work in all cases; Teams, groups, churches and their needs are unique as such careful analysis of the objective, the skills, expertise, and attitude necessary to fulfill the assignment must be considered. Let us examine the following criteria that are paramount to the selection process.

- **The Task**

This refers to the assignment to be undertaken that is all the objectives that must be completed for the vision to be realised. You need a team who is motivated and equipped to help you achieve this task.

At this stage the leader needs to ask:

- *What is my goal, or what am I trying to accomplish?*
- *What is the relationship between this and God's commission?*
- *What is needed to fulfil the assignment? (Physical and human resources)*
- *Do I have a clear focus?*
- *Is this assignment feasible?*
- *What are the milestones?*
- *How much time do I have?*
- *What skills are needed to complete this activity?*

The honest response to these questions will help the leader frame a plan that defines what is needed to complete the assignment.

▪ The Person's Traits

This refers to the individuals' traits' major characteristics. This is crucial to determine your team's commitment, especially in unfavourable seasons. It is helpful to observe if you know the person or persons personally or ask the right questions to develop an idea of the individuals before appointing them to your team or an assignment. We are also mindful that a leader sometimes inherits a team and does not have maximum control over who is on the team. However, this is also critical for determining individuals' project assignments.

Observing the individual's attitude under pressure is the best time to measure one's commitment to a task.

- *When the individual encounters challenges, is the leader tenacious or despondent?*
- *Do they attempt to improvise where resources are scarce, or do they complain?*
- *Is the person organised?*
- *Are they usually punctual and apologetic when goals are challenging to meet?*
- *Do they take responsibility, or do they make excuses?*

- *Do they use all their resources (efforts) to influence the outcome of a project?*

Positive traits will help you determine the extent to which you can depend on the individual to fulfill the assignment. Peter described the characteristics and attitude of the team member necessary for enhancing the team, group, church, or organisation's success in meeting its objectives.

Therefore, be earnest and disciplined in your prayers. Most important of all, continue to show deep love for each other, for love covers a multitude of sins. Cheerfully share your home with those who need a meal or a place to stay. God has given each of you a gift from his great variety of spiritual gifts. Use them well to serve one another. Do you have the gift of speaking? Then speak as though God himself were speaking through you. Do you have the gift of helping others? Do it with all the strength and energy that God supplies. Then everything you do will bring glory to God through Jesus Christ. **(1 Peter 4:7-11)**

Being kind, considerate, and supportive of others while working on an assignment is constructive and crucial to fulfilling the goal successfully. On the other hand, complaining about and criticising others will yield destructive outcomes, which may deter an assignment's completion.

- **The Required Knowledge and Skills**

This refers to all the knowledge and skills individuals will require to complete the assignment. Sometimes, at the initial stage, the leader or the members may not possess all the skills necessary to complete the project; however, knowing what skills or knowledge will be required to complete the project is essential. When the team leader is conscious of the necessary skills, they can outsource the required training or services. When the leader understands what needs to be done, it helps them to make critical decisions, such as outlining the roles and responsibilities of each team member from the onset. A good grasp of the project's needs helps the leader assign people based on expertise and passion, thus helping them to fulfill their roles excellently. Earlier in this chapter we examined the "Task" as this provides a practical approach to help you compile knowledge of the skills necessary for your next project. Every member of your team is valuable; there is a task that is best suited for each team member. Don't just issue assignments; assess the skills, knowledge, and passion of each member of your team, group, or church and assign them a role they can succeed at. Sometimes people fail not because they must but because of poor planning; the leader needs to give more thought to the team members and their potential. There is a place for motivating others to succeed beyond their potential. Still, even in such circumstances, the leaders inspire and encourage the individuals to excel in an area where they possess the qualities to do well, even if it's unknown personally. In such circumstances, support is needed to ensure success. The apostle Paul explained that all members are relevant in the church, have unique roles, and serve the mission differently, just as the various organs serve the human body differently. But our bodies have many parts, and God has put each part just where he wants it.

How strange a body would be if it had only one part! Yes, there are many parts, but only one body. The eye can never say to the hand, "I don't need you." The head can't say to the feet, "I don't need you. "In fact, some parts of the body that seem weakest and least important are actually the most necessary. **(1 Corinthians 12:18-19)**

The team members and their roles are essential to realising the successful outcome of an assignment. Thus, there is a need to place people where their strengths are best utilised and where they will produce maximum value. The only valid reason for appointing people to the task is competence and passion and avoiding installing people to the mission for personal preference. As you prepare to appoint members to their best-suited roles, ensure you provide them with clear task descriptions to minimise chaos or neglect. Creating a winning team is an asset for success.

- **The Individual's Background**

Being cognisant of an individual's experience and interaction can be useful. For example, within a group, an individual may have previously worked as an accountant and thus have expertise in budgeting. Therefore, the leader can appoint this person to deal with budgeting or seek guidance when handling budgeting. Thus, in addition to the person's education or training, their experience is a crucial factor to consider when selecting members for the team. We believe Jesus thought about this when He set out His plans to prepare a winning team to preach the gospel and influence others to join the Christian movement. He needed hardworking men who did not have the immediate responsibility of family but, most importantly, naturally persuasive men who knew how to fish. He foreknew that He would travel to varying places and therefore needed a team who knew how to sail, being that boat was the primary means of travel when connecting with places separated by water. He also knew that their background knowledge in fishing would help them to fulfill the intent of persuading people to serve God.

When examining an individual's background experience to generate the best team, here are some questions to ask:
- *What are your hobbies, or what do you enjoy doing?*
- *In your spare time, what do you do?*

- *What projects have you worked on before, and what roles did you play?*
- *Do you possess any other skills that might be useful to advance this assignment?*
- *What do you know about this assignment?*

Answers to these questions will be vital when considering who to appoint to your team and the role they should play in the team.

- **The Person's Values**

Although some people are skilled and credible in the area of need, they share different and conflicting core values. This can create a toxic work environment and therefore is crucial for consideration when forming your team. What drives them may affect the reputation of the mission you lead. Therefore, examine their belief system and carefully analyse the impact this has on the project, the rest of the team, and the organisation you represent. Remember,

Christ is the Chief Executive Officer for the project, and therefore the company's handbook (The Bible) should inform the team's core values. As with other organisations, all employees (team members) must adhere to the standard and exhibit a lifestyle that is in keeping with what is prescribed by the scriptures. All organisation has a handbook containing the policies that guide their members. The Bible is the final authority on determining what is acceptable; all its principles should be embraced, practiced, and enforced; it is the book of importance. It is, therefore, helpful to have an idea of the beliefs and practices of your team members before assigning them. Every member serving a church project must comprehend the missional intent of the gospel and must see themselves first as servants supporting Christ's mission.

So, whether you eat or drink, or whatever you do, do it all for the glory of God. **(1 Corinthians 10:31)**

In the same way, let your good deeds shine out for all to see so that everyone will praise your heavenly Father.

(Matthew 5:16)

 **Our actions should inspire others to join His cause and serve His mission.**

When considering the values of the individuals who will form your team, here are some questions to ask:

- *How do you treat someone who you disagree with?*
- *What is important to you when making decisions?*
- *How do you respond to negative feedback?*
- *How much do you value team input?*
- *How do you address someone who is consistently tardy?*
- *What personal qualities are essential to ensure the success of this project?*

Personal core values define an individual and give an insight into their thought process. It provides a mental picture of how individuals will interact with others and thus is paramount since teamwork requires frequent interaction to guarantee productivity. The wise man Solomon concurs.

As iron sharpens iron, so a friend sharpens a friend.

(Proverbs 27:17)

Where there are common and shared core values, a climate conducive to work will evolve, where members will encourage, support, and help each other. The team's mobilisation is critical to "winning while leading" and must be carefully undertaken. In conclusion, the following considerations are essential when pondering attracting the members to create a winning tea:

- *The Task.*
- *The individual's traits.*
- *The required knowledge and skills.*
- *The individual's background.*
- *The person's values.*

The equitable leader must recognise the talents and contributions of all team members and celebrate their differences. The equitable leader looks for ways to tap into the unique talents of others and then helps share how those talents improve the team's performance.

LEADERSHIP AND MANAGEMENT

You manage things; you lead people.
- Rear Admiral Grace

There is usually a misunderstanding between 'management' and 'leadership.' We will attempt to bring clarity. Both management and leadership are necessary to accomplish and fulfil an objective. They are intertwined and interdependent. Great leaders require excellent management skills, and superb managers must possess great leadership skills.

Who are Leaders?

Leaders possess the vision and are responsible for communicating it to the team, group, church, or organisation. Leaders set the direction, align people, and motivate people to serve. Leaders have a passion for pursuing the vision. They are committed to reaching long-term goals, taking risks to accomplish common goals, and challenging the current status quo. Leaders are responsible for motivating others to serve within the mission; they work assiduously to complete the assignment. Leaders focus on inspiration. They empower the team members, inspiring them to become future leaders. They maintain an open eye for talents and potential, redirecting followers to serve excellently. Consequently, team members follow them voluntarily.

Who are Managers?

Managers assess the tasks to be undertaken, identify and source the varying resources necessary to complete each objective, and manage the overall operation. Managers are those to whom the responsibility of management is assigned. They achieve the intended goals through excellent planning, budgeting, organisation, staffing, problem-solving, and control.

The manager aims to get the job done rather than inspire others to become leaders. Empowerment of others, if done, is so that they (the members) can enhance the project. It is, therefore, imperative to recognise that leadership and management though interrelated are two distinct and unique functions.

The Difference between Managers and Leaders

There are several definitions for the term 'leadership.' Some argue that leadership is an individual's social influence within a group. Others say that leadership entails all an individual does to influence others. Whatever your views, leaders should possess the following attributes: vision, integrity, trust, selflessness, commitment, creative ability, toughness, communication ability, risk-taking, and visibility.

On the contrary, management is a process used to accomplish organisational goals. Essentially, it is a process used to achieve what an organisation wants.

Leadership requires leaders, whereas management needs managers. The leader has the soul, passion, and creativity, while a manager has the mind, rationale, and persistence to complete the task. The leader is flexible, innovative, inspiring, courageous, and independent, while a manager is consulting, analytical, deliberate, authoritative, and stabilising.

Integrity is often associated with good leadership and is viewed as the most critical for effectiveness. Leaders are people of integrity. This involves honesty, reliability, uprightness, and honour. High-integrity leadership connects the values that a leader espouses to the actions that others see. Holding firm to what one believes, even in the most trying circumstances, is a measure of integrity. It requires consistency in the way one speaks and in one's actions. The leader with integrity holds him/herself to the same standards and expectations he/she holds others. Managers are more effective when they possess integrity. However, their focus is on the task, getting it done regardless of the cost.

The leader sees respect as essential for winning support, even among the fiercest critics. A respectful leader strives to create an environment that allows each member to produce their best work. He/she promotes cooperation, open communication, and a safer workplace. They engage consistently and appreciate similarities and differences when connected with others with different beliefs, backgrounds, or experiences. They develop a healthy curiosity to understand the perspective of others. A respectful leader is a lifelong learner who aims to display the right attitudes and behaviours to affect others positively and hold regard for others, and value them as individuals. Managers earn the confidence of others when they are relational; however, they are more concerned about the task to be completed.

Leader Vs. Manager

Leader	Manager
• Vision	• Organization
• What could be	• What is
• Alignment	• Assignment
• Motivate	• Control
• **Things get done when you're gone**	• **Things get done when you are there**
• **You have a life!!!**	• **No life!!!**

The table below will summarises the differences between the leader and the manager. It is imperative to understand whether you possess the traits of a manager vs. a leader. Both are important to the successful fulfilment of an objective. Becoming aware will help the individual to apply the right balance.

ROLES AND RESPONSIBILITY	THE MANAGER	LEADER
Vision Establishment	<ul><li>Plans and budgets.</li><li>Develops process steps and sets timelines.</li><li>Displays impersonal attitude about the vision and goals</li></ul>	<ul><li>Sets direction and develops the vision.</li><li>Develops strategic plans and achieves vision.</li><li>Displays very passionate attitude about the vision and goals</li></ul>
Human Development and Networking	<ul><li>Organises and staffs.</li><li>Maintains structure.</li><li>Delegate responsibility</li><li>Delegates authority</li><li>Implements the vision.</li><li>Establishes policy and procedures to implement vision.</li><li>Displays low emotion.</li><li>Limits team choices.</li><li>May restrict participation.</li></ul>	<ul><li>Align others with organisation goal.</li><li>Communicates the vision, mission, and direction.</li><li>Influences creation of coalitions, teams and partnerships that understand and accept the vision.</li><li>Displays driven, high emotion.</li><li>Increases choices among team members.</li></ul>

ROLES AND RESPONSIBILITY	THE MANAGER	LEADER
Vision **Execution**	- Controls processes. - Identifies problems. - Solves problems. - Monitor results. - Takes low risk approach to problem solving.	- Motivates and inspires. - Energises employees to overcome barriers to change. - Satisfies basic human needs. - Takes high risk approach to problem solving
Vision **Outcome**	- Managers vision order and predictability. - Provides expected results consistently to leadership and other stakeholders.	- Promotes useful and dramatic changes, such as new products or approaches to improving labor relations

LEADERSHIP AND ACCOUNTABILITY

Why Accountability?

"Accountability is the measure of a leader's height."
-Jeffrey Benjamin

Why is Accountability Important?

Accountability is necessary to mitigate fraud and other malpractices and encourage an environment characterised by fairness, honesty, equality, structure, and order. It could significantly reduce the time spent resolving unfulfilled expectations and other malpractices, guaranteeing success. Accountability helps improve the quality of financial reporting while promoting a healthy working culture among leaders and members alike.

What is Accountability?

Accountability is the obligation of an individual or organisation to account for its activities, accept responsibility for them, and transparently disclose the results." Accountability is taking responsibility for honest and ethical conduct towards others, and accountability is taking responsibility for one's actions, being transparent, and allowing others to observe and evaluate one's performance. All team members should be accountable to themselves and their teammates, leaders, and God. The concept of accountability runs throughout all industries, sectors, companies, professions, and churches. Accountability begins with the individual and should be implemented across departments to ensure quality service and maximum output. The leader is accountable to the church, its leaders, and others of an organisation where applicable and to God, who owns the mission and leads the assignment. Even more pronounced, we are all accountable to God since we are all stewards managing His assignment.

And I tell you this, you must give an account on judgment day for every idle word you speak. **(Matthew 12:36)**

Recognising that we are accountable to Him, we must always obey God. Every day is an opportunity to honour God through our actions, and it is actions that determine the measure of our worship. Your action matters.

Honour the Lord with thy substance, and with the first fruits of all thine increase. **(Proverbs 3:9)**

In contemporary society, companies, businesses, and other corporations develop policies that includes:
- *Holiday entitlement and conditions.*
- *Sickness/injury payment and condition.*
- *Disciplinary rules and procedures.*
- *Capability procedures.*

- *Disciplinary appeal procedure.*
- *Grievance procedure.*
- *Personal harassment policy.*
- *General information.*
- *Appointments and promotions.*

The document communicates the church, team, or group's expectations and guides the actions of members. This document is made available to all members, so this policy ensures the accountability for all members. Where a staff member violates the policy, a series of disciplinary actions may be enforced as set out in the company's policy, including an invitation to meet with the personnel committee to give an account of his/her action. Based on the findings from the hearing, one may be set free of charges, warned, punished, or dismissed. Similarly, as the leader, one should develop a church/group/team policy handbook that includes the following:

1. Policies and Procedures

This document outlines the group's goals, expectations, rules, and varying procedures, such as reporting abuse and misconduct. Scriptures should guide the policy contents, and each policy should be clear and easy to understand.

2. Policies for Leaders

This document should outline the procedures for the appointment and termination of leaders. It should set out the tenure of leadership and the procedure for an extension if he or she decides to continue to serve. This document should set out the roles and expectations of the leader. Some questions one should consider when setting up this policy are:

- *How will leaders be recruited or appointed?*
- *How will a decision be made regarding who is appointed or chosen for a leadership role?*
- *What is the job description associated with each leadership role?*
- *How will leaders be evaluated?*

- *How will leaders be compensated?*
- *What benefits will be available to leaders?*
- *What are the procedures for dealing with indiscipline?*

3. Policies regarding Treasury and Finances

This policy should specify the need for a bank account that the serving treasure and an administrative pastor should manage. There should be at least three signatories to withdraw certain amounts of cash, perhaps the treasurer or administrative pastor, a member of the board, and the senior pastor. There should be proper records of all income and expenditure. Also, regular reporting should be presented to the Board of Management monthly or quarterly. Finally, this policy should clearly state how money can be spent when it is spent, and who can authorise it. The leader should consider implementing a system for internal and external auditing to deter the misappropriation of funds. While all members should be honest, a

fundamental requirement of the Christian faith, these procedures help safeguard all, including those tasked with managing money, organisation, and the church's reputation. Some questions to consider are:
- *What qualities should the treasurer possess?*
- *Where will the money be kept?*
- *What is the maximum that should be held as petty cash?*
- *What methods will we use to collect money?*
- *How will money be accounted for?*
- *How often should reports be completed?*
- *Who should sign or authorise spending?*

4. Policies regarding Infrastructure and Property

This document should clearly outline the purposes for which the property should be used, procedures for treating and replacing damaged resources, and who is responsible for supervising the site and procuring equipment and other resources. It should also set out the purposes for which the facilities and equipment should be used and the procedure for making bookings. As you prepare your policy document consider the following:

- *Who should be responsible for the site?*
- *Who can approve an event on site?*
- *What purposes should the site be used for?*
- *What procedures are in place in the event of damage to the facility or equipment?*
- *Where should applications be made?*
- *What are the procedures for procuring equipment?*

LEADERSHIP AND ACCOUNTABILITY

Accountability and Oversight

"Exhibiting accountability over time is a gateway to trust. When we see someone acting with accountability, we gain the evidence we need to trust them."

-*Mike Erwin & Willys Devoll*

Why do We need an Oversight Body?

With the advent of independent churches (churches not part of the established and recognised entities), leaders need to set up an oversight body to monitor decision-making, manage disputes and help resolve conflicts. While having no such system may appear unharmful in the interim, it will prove necessary when disputes and conflict arise, especially if such a situation involves pastors and other influential persons within the congregation. It also becomes essential when the need arises for guidance and support, especially when difficult decisions are to be undertaken.

Benefits of an Oversight Body

In cases of severe disagreement, an oversight body can determine a timely and fair resolution. Natural justice requires an independent body to conduct hearings into controversies to encourage fairness and guard against victimisation. Fairness promotes harmony, goodwill, and a sense of equity among colleagues or members. An 'oversight body' acts as a watchdog supporting decision-making. It gives members a chance to appeal decisions, thus providing an atmosphere conducive to continuous fellowship and service because members feel the system is fair, providing recourse to disagreements. Where people feel comfortable, they are more likely to cooperate with the decisions taken even if they disagree with the outcome. This is because people think an independent body is in place to properly consider their concerns and objectively decide on the outcome. Essentially, they know a system of justice is in place, allowing them to air their concerns. Do more than implement the system; ensure it works effectively.

Within contemporary society, people often lobby for "jungle justice," a term used to describe actions taken by those not empowered to rule when they think they are mistreated. Mitigating these kinds of uprisings requires an objective committee assuring people that their concerns are heard and dealt with amicably. Even within churches, decisions sometimes appear unfair, influenced by nepotism and favouritism, especially when people feel the process is untransparent. The absence of objectivity fuels anger, dissatisfaction, and resentment leading to high attrition rates, resentment, and passive aggression.

Role of the Oversight Body

The oversight committee should be implemented to monitor the process for promotions and appointments to eliminate biases and favouritism. The leader must foster an environment where people feel they are treated fairly and impartially. They should create an environment where all people, their ideas, and perspectives of worthy of consideration. They work to give everyone a place at the organisational table. A clear description should outline the requirements for ordination, the appointment of officers, and matters requiring disciplinary actions. The process must be fair to all and should be inclusive. Where the rules and procedures are transparent and fair, hostility will be eliminated. Therefore, accountability is vital to effective leadership and management.

LEADERSHIP AND ACCOUNTABILITY

Accountability and Scripture.

"Being held accountable is an act of generosity and compassion. It is a gift that someone gives us to correct our wrongs, unlearn, and do better for the sake of our own growth. It might be uncomfortable, but it is worth the discomfort."

-Unknown

As outlined earlier in this book, God is the real leader the assignment over which we administer. Leaders are merely stewards, so we should first and foremost be guided by God's handbook for the believer, the Bible. The scripture teaches that the believer is accountable to family, colleagues, leaders, and Himself.

Believers should be Accountable to their Families.

The family is among the most influential social institutions, transmitting values, norms, beliefs, expectations, and culture. God designed it, and therefore each member has the right to hold a member of the family who functions as a leader in another institution accountable. The leader's actions highlight the family's values, and people will use their observation of the leader to form an idea of the family. Therefore, the leader is accountable to the family and, therefore, must reflect the standards and practices of the family as outlined in the scripture below.

This is a trustworthy saying: "If someone aspires to be a church leader, he desires an honorable position." So, a church leader must be a man whose life is above reproach. He must be faithful to his wife. He must exercise self-control, live wisely, and have a good reputation. He must enjoy having guests in his home, and he must be able to teach. He must not be a heavy drinker or be violent. He must be gentle, not quarrelsome, and not love money. He must manage his own family well, having children who respect and obey him. For if a man cannot manage his own household, how can he take care of God's church?

(1 Timothy 3:1-5)

Members should be Accountable to Each other

We are interdependent and, therefore, must rely on the conscious guidance, advice, and support of others. It is often said, "No man is an island, and no man stands alone." The constructive criticism of others is a mirror that shows what needs to change, improve, or be discontinued. Without these revelations, one is at risk of continuing along with moral destruction.

So, stop telling lies. Let us tell our neighbors the truth, for we are all parts of the same body. And "don't sin by letting anger control you." Don't let the sun go down while you are still angry, for anger gives a foothold to the devil. If you are a thief, quit stealing. Instead, use your hands for good hard work, and then give generously to others in need. Don't use foul or abusive language. Let everything you say be good and helpful, so that your words will be an encouragement to those who hear them. And do not bring sorrow to God's Holy Spirit by the way you live. Remember, he has identified you as his own, guaranteeing that you will be saved on the day of redemption. Get rid of all bitterness, rage, anger, harsh words, and slander, as well as all types of evil behavior. Instead, be kind to each other, tenderhearted, forgiving one another, just as God through Christ has forgiven you. **(Ephesians 4:25-32)**

Believers should be Accountable to Leaders

In addition to submitting to the wisdom of peers, one must be accountable to those in leadership. Not only is this a good relationship, but it is Godly, and it reflects the orderly nature of our God and should be practiced minimising chaos and confusion in our daily operations.

Obey your leaders and submit to them, for they are keeping watch over your souls, as those who will have to give an account. Let them do this with joy and not with groaning, for that would be of no advantage to you.

(Hebrews 13:17)

Believers should be Accountable to God

God owns the project while we are the temporary managers serving specific objectives. Therefore, we must prepare to give God an account concerning our stewardship.

And no creature is hidden from his sight, but all are naked and exposed to the eyes of him to whom we must give account. *(Hebrews 4:13)*

The Body of Christ is Interconnected

The Body of Christ is interconnected, and we have a duty to each other to build each other up. Encouragement and moral support from a friend, teammate, or family member are sometimes missing in fighting the battle against dishonesty and other malpractices. Proverbs 27:17 occurs, "Iron sharpens iron; so, a man sharpens his friend's countenance." Being accountable to one another can provide those missing ingredients to becoming a disciplined and effective leader, and accountability can be helpful in the battle to overcome sin. Consider this statement by Apostle James: "Confess your sins to each other and pray for each other so that you may be healed. The prayer of a righteous person is powerful and effective" (James 5:16). Being conscious of our ongoing battle against the forces of darkness, we should gather all the help we can see around us, and this may include making ourselves accountable to another believer, family member or teammate who can encourage us in the fight. Do everything to ensure we are honest and fair in all our dealings.

LEADERSHIP AND ACCOUNTABILITY

The Leader, Responsibility and Accountability?

"Leaders inspire accountability through their ability to accept responsibility before they place blame."
                                        -Courtney Lynch

- **Accountability Begins with the Leader**

The leader/manager is responsible for defining and creating a culture of accountability. Some ways the leader/manager can demonstrate by:

✓ *Taking ownership of the vision.*

✓ *Being responsible.*

✓ *Being punctual.*

✓ *Meeting deadlines.*

✓ *Offering an apology when deadlines are not met.*

- **Accountability is a Recurring Activity**

This means the leader should consistently lead by example and hold others accountable always. *It is easier to lighten up than to tighten up – **Unknown**.*

- **Accountability should be Applied to All**

Everyone should be held accountable by the same standards, including the leader. As a leader, arrange varying review sessions with your teams with the view to:

✓ *Providing clarity to members of their role, responsibility, and expectation.*

✓ *Provide feedback support.*

✓ *Offer praise and encouragement to move people further if things are going well.*

- **Accountability Cannot be Delegated**

As the leader, you should be fair and hold all team members accountable. The expectations must be clear. This responsibility cannot be passed on or handed down to others. Whereas the leader can delegate assignments, the responsibility of ensuring that it is down to a high standard remains the sole duty of the leader. Others can help to get the work done; however, the leader must ensure the objectives are met. Accountability must be active and not passive. Accountability is not micromanagement; it does not have to make people uncomfortable. Accountability does not have to be confrontational; if administered well, it is something even the laziest team member will appreciate. Communicate the standards clearly, train and equip your team to excel at the standards and appreciate them when they do. When the team respects you, they will work hard to meet your expectations.

- **Accountability is the Difference Between Success and Failure**

Leadership keeps leaders in sync with purpose and consistently reminds them of the objective of God's mission. Accountability rejects mediocrity and discourages complacency. It reinforces the vision and encourages the involvement of all members of the team. It entails frequent monitoring and detailed evaluation for all team members highlighting strengths and weaknesses with the view of encouraging continuous improvement. Each team member is an advisor against all forms of malpractice. At the same time, each is responsible for constant improvement to maximise the overall realisation of the mission. The wisest man of all time, Solomon posits *"plans go wrong for lack of advice; many advisers bring success.* **(Proverbs 15:22)**

Accountability Safeguards

Accountability is vital to the successful operation of a company and must be implemented and enforced at all levels of the institution. Each team member is first and foremost accountable to God and therefore is expected to serve all assignments as on to God. Members of the institution are also accountable to each other (leaders and peers) and their families.

Accountability safeguards against malpractices and promotes good values among each team member.

LEADERSHIP, PROFESSIONAL &SPIRITUAL DEVELOPMENT

Success is not final; failure is not fatal: It is the courage to continue that counts.
-Winston S. Churchill

With the advent of new technology and the multiple evolving processes for getting tasks done, team members must engage in lifelong learning, which is the only way to provide cutting-edge services and complete assignments at world-class standards in an efficient manner. This approach to leadership and management happens in the corporate world and should not be forsaken in our churches if we are to deliver the best programs. Constant learning creates the opportunity to satisfy the growing demands, which will guarantee productivity, efficiency, and sometimes convenience to both members of the team and those you serve or engage with. This type of training and skill development is called professional development.

What is Professional Development?

This refers to leaders and team members **expanding** and improving their **skills** to meet the needs of their assignment and those they serve. There are several approaches that the leader can consider deciding how to improve the skills and knowledge of the team. Professional development may entail:

- *reviewing case studies,*
- *consultation and coaching,*
- *mentoring,*
- *technical assistance.*

The leader should constantly conduct frequent audits to determine the skills and knowledge necessary to improve the service, task, or assignment objectives. Once the leader assesses the task, he or she must begin to create a plan that will help the team acquire the skills needed to be proficient and effective. The plan is called a professional development plan.

What is a Professional Development Plan?

A Professional Development Plan is the roadmap containing the skills, strategy, and education you need to further your career and life to achieve your professional goals. In essence, it outlines the goals for the individual as a member of the team and a list of steps to achieve them. It can also aid you in identifying and developing the professional skills needed to reach your goals and keep you on track to success.

Who should Create a Professional Develop Plan?

As leader/manager of the team, one of your core responsibilities is to empower the members and sharpen their skills to enhance their performance as it relates to their role and the assignment to be completed. A professional development plan is created by the manager working closely with the staff member to identify the necessary skills and resources to support the staff member's career goals and the organisation's business needs."

How to Make a Professional Development Plan?

Martinelli (2017) recommends the ensuing 9 steps to consider when completing a PDP:

- *Assess where you are now.*
- *Identify your specific career goals.*
- *Gather information.*
- *Identify what professional skills you already have and which you need to work on.*
- *Choose how you will accomplish your goals.*

- *Develop a timeline for accomplishing your specific targets and goals.*
- *Write it all down.*
- *Evaluate your plan.*
- *Measure your progress.*

LEADERSHIP AND CHANGE

"Everyone thinks to change the world. No one thinks to change himself."

-Albert Schweitzer

Leaders are responsible for bringing about change without any direct or apparent effort. As an agent of change, the leader must be encouraging, inspirational, proactive, visionary, and industrious. This involves inspiring those you lead to be confident in their abilities and contributions. Change is inevitable. It cannot be avoided but must be embraced. Growth is only achievable and possible with modifications. Adapting to change is crucial for both development and survival. It is not necessarily the strongest or the fittest that survive but the ones who can adapt to changes. Change, though necessary, if it is too sudden. It can cause more harm than no change at all. The leader that introduces changes must be aware of the people's physical and mental ability and clinically and wisely provide the support and guidance that will allow them to do so in a timely fashion to reach the goal. The purpose of change must always be to achieve results but must consider the human element.

Leaders must recognise the need for and possess the grit and determination to lead individuals and organisations through the 'change' process. Leadership must be able to adjust both the style and targets where necessary. Change is an essential feature of growth, and living and dynamic things, such as people, will grow through change. We become better after we master the discomforts that come with change. The process of change will require access to opportunity despite the challenges.

Leadership is not the exercise of power but the empowerment of people. The focus of leadership must be empowering people to achieve results that benefit the group. The wise leader will empower rather than be intimidated by those he leads. The team members should complement and refrain from competing. The wise leader will surround him/herself with those who are teachable, accountable, and committed to the vision. The art of empowerment lies in mobilising, training, empowering, and maintaining the people to fulfil the vision.

Leadership is never static but a dynamic process. In many instances, adjustments must be made based on the changing realities within which leadership is done. The number one asset that any leader has is the people, and management should consider how they manage resources and people's expectations. Change can result in an unsettling period because of the initial uncertainties, especially if it is a major change in direction. However, the leader's confidence, openness, and a clear line of communication can allay the fears and maintain the drive toward fulfilling the goal.

Why is there Resistance to Change?

- *Ignorant of the value. If the need to change is not clearly understood or the perceived importance is not understood, there may be an unwillingness to invest resources.*
- *Uncomfortable with the strategies being employed.*
- *Vision not clear.*
- *Lack of transparency from leadership.*
- *Lack of Commitment.*
- *Poor Communication.*
- *Fear of the Unknown.*
- *Unwillingness to give up existing benefits and beliefs.*
- *Awareness of the weaknesses in the proposed changes.*
- *Feelings of Insecurity.*

- *Resource Limitations.*

Even Good ideas that will positively impact the church, group, or team may be resisted if they involve a significant alteration in how things are done and if it is poorly introduced. The leader must communicate well and be sensitive to the team's feelings. Leadership must therefore be cognisant of where the people are and progress at a pace that will deliver the intended outcome while reassuring those being led.

Vital Steps to Consider in Leading Change

- *Create an awareness of the Urgency of the Change:*
- *Mobilise others around the essential need for the change.*
- *Develop a clear and strategic plan.*
- *Select and train those that can influence participation.*
- *Monitor both the inputs and outcomes.*

The necessity for change can be precipitated mainly during a time of crisis. The leader must, therefore, properly analyse the situation and make the adequate adjustments needed to face the eventuality. In leading change, one of the greatest assets of the leader will be clarity in communication. Lack of clarity can lead to misunderstanding and confusion. Great leaders tend to navigate through the delicate balance of being people or task oriented. The reality is that leading through change is only possible with the assistance of the team. The team that possesses confidence in the leader's ability and objective will be far more cooperative and less resistant to the changes being implemented. This would make for greater harmony and cohesion in the working relationship.

The heart of change requires doing things differently to yield the appropriate results or achieve the requisite goals.

LEADERSHIP CHARACTER AND INTEGRITY

"Integrity lies in, doing what one speaks; speaking what one does."

-M. K. Soni

Of all Christian characteristics, integrity should never be compromised. It is the quality of honesty and trustworthiness. It requires the leader and team to adhere to a robust set of principles grounded in the scriptural teachings of Christ. Integrity gives people power, particularly the group leader, to take responsibility for their actions. Integrity demands that leaders remain true to their values and principles as defined by the leader's handbook, the Bible. The most crucial thing is always to behave honestly and consistently, no matter what. When leaders demonstrate integrity and trustworthiness, their teams are often inspired to have confidence in them because they can be relied upon to do what they say they will do. It is effortless to believe in leadership that is reliable, loyal, dependable, and worthy of trust. Leaders with integrity can have a lasting impression on the team, group, organisation, church, its members, and other stakeholders who rely on the services. They also help set a positive tone within a company by acting according to its values.

It is the expectation that all Spiritual leaders possess and demonstrate integrity, honesty, and adherence to a pattern of good works." Leaders are first Christians, and people called to obey God and, in so doing, to be people of uncompromised morality and integrity. Christians should be those who adhere to the truth and who do good works.

Therefore, since God in his mercy has given us this new way, we never give up. We reject all shameful deeds and underhanded methods. We don't try to trick anyone or distort the word of God. We tell the truth before God, and all who are honest know this. **(2 Corinthians 4:1-2)**

Leaders must demonstrate a life of integrity, honesty, and exemplary living, one worth being imitated by others. They should be the epitome of what they teach and preach. Leaders are people of upright character. Upright character is essential to the leader's life; it guards one's reputation. It is a necessity for success in any sphere of life. Without it, nations, businesses, churches, and families crumble and fall into moral disarray. Character is informed by integrity and integrity by the principles of the Word of God.

" The way of the Lord is strength to the upright."

(Proverbs 10:29)

Christians should be like Jesus bearing the conduct of a believer. In Christ, we are new creations without blemish (deception, manipulation, dishonesty) before God.

Leaders must never use the word of God for deceit or personal gain. God's word must never be used as a snare or a yoke to keep those we lead in bondage but rather model the expected behaviour. Integrity is moral soundness or uprightness.

 **Integrity denotes living what you preach and preaching what you live.**

There must be a rejection of all shameful and dishonest deeds and dealings. The leader must avoid practices that can bring disgrace or cause a scandal. These should have no part in the life of the godly leader, and this will call for personal introspection. The leader's life must be open and above board to ensure that his/her conduct does not reproach him/her, their family, or the message they preach. There should be a blatant rejection of all immoral practices, covetousness, impure thoughts, and unbridled selfish ambitions that can lead to corruption.

The spiritual leader must not succumb to trickery, cunning craftiness, and shrewd behaviour with an intent of evil. It should never be the objective to endeavour to do anything and use any means to get what you want. The misuse and abuse of personnel are not Christ-like and should be avoided at all costs. The leader's lifestyle must follow both patterns and radiate the virtues of Christ from the heart.

The Word of God should never be distorted for personal advantage. The leader must always remember whom he/she represents and maintain high standards. Leaders are God's spokespersons and, as such, must never falsify the word of God or mishandle it in such a way as to deceive and ensnare others. Extreme caution must be exercised so that the word of God is not adulterated by customs and traditions or used out of context to support beliefs and ideologies or for exploitation.

The truth must be proclaimed with all sincerity and honesty. There should be no hidden motives or desire to manipulate or deceive in its declaration.

DEMONSTRATING AND PRESERVING INTEGRITY

"If you don't stand for something you will fall for anything."

-Gordon A. Eadie

The previous chapter explores what integrity means for leadership. We will examine how integrity can be demonstrated and preserved and its benefits.

Integrity is preserved when we:

- **Keep your Commitment**

The leader must ensure that he honours his/her word. Once a task is undertaken, it must be continued to the end. Leaders should demonstrate dedication in pursuit of their objectives.

- **Be Fair in Your Dealings**

This ensures that the leader is conforming to both Godly and ethical practices. Behaviours that reek of dishonesty and deception should always be avoided to evade a tainted reputation. This requires honesty at all points to build trust and foster good relationships.

- **Be Transparent and Direct in Communication.**

Ensure that you are honest and unambiguous in your remarks as the leader.

- **Willingness to Acknowledge Mistakes**

It is sometimes possible to make mistakes or err in judgment. When this happens, one must accept responsibility for his/her actions and seek to correct them by admission and, where possible, restitution. It is never a good thing to blame others for bad decision-making.

- **Give Credit where it is Due**

The leader must desist from plagiarism both in writing and speaking. Be sure to acknowledge the work and worth of others.

- **Avoid Cutting Corners**

The easiest way might not be the best way. Always consider before acting and weigh your decisions with God's word.

- **Do not Mislead**

Do not mislead people Through False Declarations. This is tantamount to not speaking the truth to give the wrong impression.

- **Do not Lie to Yourself or to Others**

This is at the heart of being transparent. Speaking and adhering to the truth and never compromising on Godly values.

How do We Preserve Integrity?

- *Practice keeping your word.*
- *Develop habits that place you above reproach.*
- *Avoid situations where there is a conflict of interest.*
- *Be honest in all your financial undertakings.*
- *Do not make promises that you have no intention of keeping or are unable to keep.*
- *Make better choices.*
- *Do not under ask and over expect.*
- *Be above board in all your dealings.*
- *Be honest as it relates to your opinions.*

The Benefits of a Lifestyle of Integrity

- Integrity is the prescription for establishing and maintaining healthy relationships, making individuals want to work with and be around you.

- Integrity allows you to be confident in your approach to life without having to keep looking over your shoulders because of dishonourable conduct or behaviour. You, therefore, have no fear that the unsavoury aspects of your past will catch up with you.

- Your life becomes more meaningful. You approach life with a definite sense of purpose because you have something meaningful and exemplary to contribute.

- You become an invaluable asset as an example and a mentor in guiding others.

- A life of integrity protects you from false accusations because your character will speak volumes on your behalf. The truth will always cause you to win because what you say is who you are.

- You can be proud of your advances and achievements, knowing that nothing untoward was done.

- You become trustworthy, and those who interact with you understand that you will not manipulate or deceive them into furthering selfish ambitions.

- Your lifestyle not only witnesses to the work of Christ within your life but is attractive to those needing a transformation in theirs.

- It will provide excellent opportunities for you in life because you will be seen as dependable.

- The principles that govern your decision-making are based on transparency and ethical considerations. It is, therefore, easy for you to be consistent in your approach irrespective of the levels of difficulties.

- Above all, God is pleased with this lifestyle that will honour Him.

 Remember that integrity is choosing your thoughts and actions based on values rather than personal gain always.

PRAYER AND LEADERSHIP

Prayer lays hold of God's plan and becomes the link between his will and its accomplishment on earth. Amazing things happen, and we are given the privilege of being the channels of the Holy Spirit's prayer.

-Elisabeth Elliot

It is possible to lead without prayer; however, prayer must undergird its operation concerning Spiritual Organisations. The leader, therefore, must recognise that prayer is not optional and must be deemed his/her number one priority if he/she is to provide Spiritual Leadership and oversight. Jesus exemplified the importance of prayer as an integral part of his leadership model. Despite the rigors and demands of ministry, he would withdraw to fellowship with God in prayer. In many instances, He would be alone and would pray for prolonged periods. Jesus' commitment to prayer was directly connected to his relationship with God.

One day soon afterward Jesus went up on a mountain to pray, and he prayed to God all night. **(Luke 6:12)**

Lead in Prayer by Precept and Example

The Godly leader recognises that prayer must not only be taught but it must also be modelled. This modeling of prayer must be clear to all that is being led. What you teach becomes more effective when it is observed as a regular part of your lifestyle. Jesus' disciples were eager to learn how to pray when they observed him praying and were also aware that John had taught his disciples to pray.

Once Jesus was in a certain place praying. As he finished, one of his disciples came to him and said, "Lord, teach us to pray, just as John taught his disciples. **(Luke 11:1)**

Jesus as the greater teacher, both practiced and modeled the behaviour that he wanted his disciples to pattern.

 **The distinctive of prayer is best taught, not caught.**

Lead the Church/Group in Prayer

The leader must be the principal prayer leader within the church, a responsibility that must not be delegated. Others can be trained to assist; however, they have the full responsibility of guiding the church in this most sacred aspect of their spiritual journey. Jesus refers to the church as a House of Prayer for all nations. Therefore, the spiritual leader is responsible for guiding the church in this most vital of the Spiritual disciplines.

He said to them, "The Scriptures declare, 'My Temple will be called a house of prayer for all nations,' but you have turned it into a den of thieves. **(Mark 11:17)**

The scriptures are replete with examples of spiritual leaders who publicly led the people in prayer. It was seen as part of their corporate responsibility and held with great regard. Solomon prayed at the temple's dedication, Jehoshaphat prayed when faced with the threat of advancing enemies, and David prayed after the Philistines had raided Ziklag, burned it with fire, and taken the people captive.

Personal Prayer Life

Prayer is deemed one of the most intimate spiritual encounters with God and is vital for strengthening our (leader and God) relationship. Unlike other types of leadership, prayer is an essential part of the core values of those engaged in the work of the Lord. Spiritual leaders are not exempt from making this personal commitment and must seek to do this regularly. Quality times are deemed necessary and must become a regular part of the leader's schedule. Personal time with God must never be replaced or sidelined because of other ministerial responsibilities. The leader's prayer life is not only essential but also his number one priority and irreplaceable. The Spiritual leader should never talk to men about God until they have spoken to God about men.

And we are confident that he hears us whenever we ask for anything that pleases him. And since we know he hears us when we make our requests, we also know that he will give us what we ask for. ***(1 John 5:14-15)***

The leader's personal devotion and quiet time are a must, and they should not be done simply out of a sense of duty but primarily out of love and conviction. The desire to pray must spring from intrinsic motivation and passion, and the leader must model his prayer life based on the teachings of Christ. Prayer is a significant way of maintaining communication with God, which revolves around speaking and listening to hear what God has to say. The leader's relationship with God is intricately tied to his/her prayer life. All spiritual leaders must be persons of prayer. The leader's prayer life must be done in solitude, where there is a quiet reflection and the building of intimacy with God, but also in the corporate setting, which will inspire those being led to recognise the priority of prayer and be prompted to do the same. A significant ministry is always accomplished when the believers receive the prayers of their leaders.

The earnest prayer of a righteous person has great power and produces wonderful results. **(James 5:16b)**

PRAYER, SELECTION, APPOINTMENT AND MAINTENANCE OF WORKERS

"Any concern too small to be turned into prayer is too small to be made into a burden."

-Corrie Ten Bloom

An integral part of organisational growth and development revolves around staff selection. Great caution must be exercised in this selection process. Jesus prayed all night before he selected the disciples that would be trained to continue the mission later. Jesus demonstrated that prayer was vital to making the right decision in leadership selection and succession.

One day soon afterward Jesus went up on a mountain to pray, and he prayed to God all night. 13At daybreak he called together all his disciples and chose twelve of them to be apostles. **(Luke 6:12-13)**

Prayer was a natural part of the routine of the Apostles post resurrection. The selection of Matthias to replace Judas was made after a period of intense prayer. The prayer was specific and requested of God his direct involvement in the selection process.

Then they all prayed, "O Lord, you know every heart. Show us which of these men you have chosen as an apostle to replace Judas in this ministry, for he has deserted us and gone where he belongs." **(Luke 1:24-25)**

Prayer and Administration

The Apostles did not see a rigid dichotomy between *prayer* and *administration* but recognised the importance of seeking God in governing the

Church's affairs. The selection criteria were borne out of their continuous devotion and commitment to prayer. Devotion to the word of God and Prayer did not affect proper administrative decision-making but allowed for continued spiritual expansion of the work. All administrative decision-making was ratified by prayer as those chosen to lead were confirmed in their respective appointments. Prayerful consideration must be given to all aspects of decision-making.

So, the Twelve called a meeting of all the believers. They said, "We apostles should spend our time teaching the word of God, not running a food program. And so, brothers, select seven men who are well respected and are full of the Spirit and wisdom. We will give them this responsibility. Then we apostles can spend our time in prayer and teaching the word. "Everyone liked this idea, and they chose the following: Stephen (a man full of faith and the Holy Spirit), Philip, Procorus, Nicanor, Timon,

Parmenas, and Nicolas of Antioch (an earlier convert to the Jewish faith). These seven were presented to the apostles, who prayed for them as they laid their hands on them. **(Acts 6:2-6)**

DEVELOPING A CULTURE OF PRAYING

The prayer level of a church never rises any higher than the personal example and passion of the leaders. The quantity and quality of prayer in leadership meetings is the essential indicator of the amount of prayer that will eventually arise among the congregation.
-Daniel Henderson

Developing a culture of prayer must be seen as a significant aspect of the leader's responsibility. Not only must he be passionate about prayer, but he must also motivate others to be consistent in their endeavour to pray. Implicit in this is recognising God as the source and a willingness to submit to his will. The sacrifice and commitment of a leader to pray tend to be contagious, resulting in the church functioning as a house of prayer for all.

Leaders must lead by both precept and example. A primary distinctive of the early church was the passion and devotion exhibited by the leadership to prayer. They saw it as an absolute necessity and made it their priority.

They all met together and were constantly united in prayer, along with Mary the mother of Jesus, several other women, and the brothers of Jesus. **(Acts 1:14)**

All the believers devoted themselves to the apostles' teaching, and to fellowship, and to sharing in meals (including the Lord's Supper), and to prayer. **(Acts 2:42)**

This culture of prayer provided for boldness in Christian witness, an explosion of miracles and healings, strong fellowship and bonding among the believers, and a significant impact on society.

"Every leader knows the skills in which they excel. They also are aware of those tasks that they maintain a certain level of competence along with those duties they struggle to accomplish. In my experience there are "want to's" and the "have to's" of leadership. The "want to's" energise a leader and the "have to's" zap the leader's creativity and time. The quicker a leader can fill the gaps of their weaknesses, the more effective they will be in achieving God's mission." — <u>Gary Rohrmayer</u>

Prayer helps the leader to distinguish between the things he/she must do and those he/she should avoid pursuing. When the leader practice to pray about everything, he/she will inspire others to the same.

For more information on effective praying, consider getting our book on prayer.
- **Critical Keys for Effective Praying**

THE LEADERSHIP, GOD'S WORD, AND THE CHURCH

Work hard so you can present yourself to God and receive his approval. Be a good worker, one who does not need to be ashamed and who correctly explains the word of truth.
-2 Timothy 2:15

Strong Spiritual leadership must have at its core an understanding and application of the word of God. The word of God must govern all matters related to faith and practice. The spiritual leader is a student of the word and allows God's message to provide guidance. All leaders must subscribe to the philosophy of being lifelong learners following the examples of the Apostles:

"Gave themselves to pray and study the word."

(Acts 6:4)

The leader must ensure that the Word is correctly understood within its context and applied personally, then by extension, to those he/she leads. The Word of God cannot be minimised, overemphasised, or subsidised because it is the predominant resource for edification, empowerment, and guidance. The leader must be able to thoroughly exegete and apply the scriptures contextually when dealing with leadership matters such as developing rules and regulations for the church, managing conflicts, and decision-making. In matters where the Bible is vague, the leader should be vague; however, where the Bible is explicit, the leader must be willing to conform and lead the people. Whereas opinions may be valuable to the successful operation of the church as an institution, the Bible must be the foundational reference tool; therefore, all opinions should be measured by the total weight of the scriptures.

And the people of Berea were more open-minded than those in Thessalonica, and they listened eagerly to Paul's message. They searched the Scriptures Day after day to see if Paul and Silas were teaching the truth. ***(Acts 17:11)***

Therefore, the Bible is God's direct voice to His church (or sub-group) and must inform our practices. The leader should never be offended by the verification checks made by those being taught concerning matters relating to the scriptures. The learners should be commended for the diligence being exercised. If what is being taught by the Word is true, it should be left open to scrutiny and reexamination.

 **The truth will withstand the test.**

The Word of God reflects the very heart and character of leadership as epitomised by the master teacher/leader. Jesus emphasised that the highest level of leadership is not being served but being of service to others. The leadership style of Jesus was both servanthood and relational.

Then they began to argue among themselves about who would be the greatest among them. Jesus told them, "In this world the kings and great men lord it over their people, yet they are called 'friends of the people.' But among you it will be different. Those who are the greatest among you should take the lowest rank, and the leader should be like a servant. Who is more important, the one who sits at the table or the one who serves? The one who sits at the table, of course. But not here! For I am among you as one who serves. **(Luke 22:24-27)**

The leader's message must be grounded in the Word of God and contain elements of rebuke, reproof, correction, and instruction. This will shape the believer's faith and conviction.

Preach the word of God. Be prepared, whether the time is favorable or not. Patiently correct, rebuke, and encourage your people with good teaching. **(2 Timothy 4:2)**

The leader must trust the Word of God and not depend upon worldly observation, research, and perspectives to lead the people. Whereas worldly observation, research, and people's ideas can be helpful they must be discarded if they contradict God's Word. Trusting the Word of God will leave little to no room for syncretism, that is, incorporating other beliefs to make the gospel or the message more appealing. The reliance on charisma, theatrics, and new-era approaches to influence people's decision-making is erroneous and should be avoided by the Christ-led Church.

We reject all shameful deeds and underhanded methods. We don't try to trick anyone or distort the word of God. We tell the truth before God, and all who are honest know this. **(2 Corinthians 4:2)**

The Bible is enough to convict, support, edify, and guide the believer. The Bible (Word of God) is the primary tool of deliverance and therefore takes precedence over all other methods.

Preach the word of God. Be prepared, whether the time is favorable or not. Patiently correct, rebuke, and encourage your people with good teaching. **(2 Timothy 4:2)**

The Bible is complete, and no other additive is necessary. Leaders are called to implement the scriptural imperatives without adding, removing, or misrepresenting its content.

And I solemnly declare to everyone who hears the words of prophecy written in this book: If anyone adds anything to what is written here, God will add to that person the plagues described in this book. And if anyone removes any of the words from this book of prophecy, God will remove that person's share in the tree of life and in the holy city that are described in this book. **(Revelation 22:18-19)**

The Word of God represents God's authority in the world and is effective in every jurisdiction across the globe and can cause tremendous impact.

His command is backed by great power. No one can resist or question it. **(Ecclesiastes 8:4)**

The Bible is God's Road map and is timeless in its applicability, and it must be consulted on all matters of human behaviour and conduct.

Your words are a lamp to guide my feet and a light for my path. **(Psalm 119:105)**

If sin is the virus, God's Word is the vaccine to effect the cure. It deals with a wide range of human shortcomings providing the prescription for wholeness.

I have hidden your word in my heart that I might not sin against you. **(Psalms 119:11)**

The Word of God represents the highest standard for guiding human behaviour and has been approved and endorsed by the highest authority in the universe, God Himself.

I will worship toward thy holy temple and praise thy name for thy lovingkindness and for thy truth: for thou hast magnified thy word above all thy name. **(Psalms 138:2)**

The Word of God is useful to produce faith. All things present are the result of God's spoken word, and the Word of God is a prerequisite necessary for faith construction.

By the word of the Lord were the heavens made; and all the host of them by the breath of his mouth. **(Psalms 33:6)**

The Word of God is immutable and perfect in that it is tried and proven.

The words of the Lord are pure words: as silver tried in a furnace of earth, purified seven times. **(Psalms 12:6)**

Alignment with scriptural teaching is the determining factor of the trueness of a church. What is mentioned in scripture is the Word of God is to be the guide that the church follow.

And now I commend you to God [placing you in His protective, loving care] and [I commend you] to the word of His grace [the counsel and promises of His unmerited favor]. His grace is able to build you up and to give you the [rightful] inheritance among all those who are sanctified [that is, among those who are set apart for God's purpose—all believers]. **(Acts 20:32, AMP)**

Scripture is the infallible measuring stick for all our doctrines and practices.

All Scripture is God-breathed [given by divine inspiration] and is profitable for instruction, for conviction [of sin], for correction [of error and restoration to obedience], for training in righteousness [learning to live in conformity to God's will, both publicly and privately—behaving honorably with personal integrity and moral courage]; so that the man of God may be complete and proficient, outfitted and thoroughly equipped for every good work. **(2 Tim 3:16-17, AMP)**

Scriptures is the standard by which we compare our practices.

The brothers immediately sent Paul and Silas away by night to Berea; and when they arrived, they entered the Jewish synagogue. Now these people were more noble and open-minded than those in Thessalonica, so they received the message [of salvation through faith in the Christ] with great eagerness, examining the Scriptures daily to see if these things were so. As a result, many of them became believers, together with a number of prominent Greek women and men.

(Acts 17:10-12, AMP)

Apostolic authority was passed on through the apostles' writings, not through apostolic succession. Scripture's support supports the word of God being prime ingredient for equipping leaders and members alike.

Succession planning must be an integral part of the continuation of Spiritual leadership. There is a need to deposit into the lives of people to continue the work once established.

You have heard me teach things that have been confirmed by many reliable witnesses. Now teach these truths to other trustworthy people who will be able to pass them on to others. **(2 Timothy 2:2)**

For more information on using God's Word effectively, consider getting our books on biblical interpretation:
- **Critical Keys for Biblical Interpretation Vol 1 & 2**

THE LEADER AND THE HOLY SPIRIT

And I will ask the Father, and he will give you another Advocate, who will never leave you. He is the Holy Spirit, who leads into all truth. The world cannot receive him, because it isn't looking for him and doesn't recognise him. But you know him, because he lives with you now and later will be in you.

-John 14:16-17

The Holy Spirit is the primary advisor to the leader, and therefore the leader must seek and rely on His leadership. The Holy Spirit is of more value than only 'speaking in tongues', or an entity called on to show forth our potency. He was given as the helper (parakletos), meaning He was given to assist someone else as an advisor, legal defender, mediator, and intercessor. Being aware of this reality, the leader must never attempt to decide or rule on any matter without first consulting the Holy Spirit. He has the final ruling on any matter regarding His people and the church, and such leaders should lead Christ's church based on the advice of the Holy Spirit. Therefore, the Holy Spirit is the Spirit of Truth and will never contradict the Word of Truth. His role is to reveal the truth and bring clarity to the leader relating to scripture and other situations that demand leadership.

He is the Holy Spirit, who leads into all truth.
(John 14:17a)

The Holy Spirit does not instill fear or cause people to become afraid. The leader led by the Holy Spirit is confident, bold, and disciplined and distances him or herself from situations that lead to or encourage fear in the community he/she serves. Instead, his role is to lead in love and promote sound reasoning.

For God has not given us a spirit of fear and timidity, but of power, love, and self-discipline. **(2 Timothy 1:7)**

The leader must remain in fellowship with the Holy Spirit to resist the desire for sin. Maintaining a relationship with the Holy Spirit means the Holy Spirit can reside in, preside over, and influence the leader. He/she makes him/herself vulnerable to the extent that the Holy Spirit primarily influences him/her, and he/she will pattern his/her action based on the directives of the Holy Spirit.

Let the Holy Spirit guide your lives. Then you won't be doing what your sinful nature craves. The sinful nature wants to do evil, which is just the opposite of what the Spirit wants. And the Spirit gives us desires that are the opposite of what the sinful nature desires. These two forces are constantly fighting each other, so you are not free to carry out your good intentions. **(Galatian 5:16-18)**

The Holy Spirit is demonstrated in the quality of the leader's life and is not merely the presence of gifts. The Holy Spirit must, therefore, not only reside but preside. A life in which the Holy Spirit reigns is outlined in the text below.

But the fruit of the Spirit is love, joy, peace, forbearance, kindness, goodness, faithfulness, gentleness, and self-control. **(Galatians 5:22-23)**

The Holy Spirit furnishes the church with gifts and not the leader. These gifts were given to edify the church; therefore, the leader develops an appreciation for demonstrating these gifts and should not be intimidated. If the Holy Spirit gives it, it is necessary to advance the church.

A spiritual gift is given to each of us so we can help each other. To one person the Spirit gives the ability to give wise advice; to another the same Spirit gives a message of special knowledge. The same Spirit gives great faith to another, and to someone else the one Spirit gives the gift of healing. He gives one person the power to perform miracles, and another the ability to prophesy. He gives someone else the ability to discern whether a message is from the Spirit of God or from another spirit. Still another person is given the ability to speak in unknown languages, while another is given the ability to interpret what is being said. It is the one and only Spirit who distributes all these gifts. He alone decides which gift each person should have.

(1 Corinthians 12:7-11)

The Holy Spirit oversees the appointment and delegation of responsibility to leaders. The task of feeding and shepherding God's people is primary and foremost.

So, guard yourselves and God's people. Feed and shepherd God's flock—his church, purchased with his own blood—over which the Holy Spirit has appointed you as leaders.

(Acts 20:28)

One day as these men were worshiping the Lord and fasting, the Holy Spirit said, "Appoint Barnabas and Saul for the special work to which I have called them.

(Acts 13:2)

The Holy Spirit was given to promote Christ and not the leader's personal agenda.

But you will receive power when the Holy Spirit comes upon you. And you will be my witnesses, telling people about me everywhere—in Jerusalem, throughout Judea, in Samaria, and to the ends of the earth." **(Acts 1:8)**

The leader must never rely on his own expertise but on the ability of the Holy Spirit.

Then he said to me, "This is the word of the Lord to Zerubbabel: Not by might, nor by power, but by my Spirit, says the Lord of hosts. **(Zechariah 4:6)**

The Holy Spirit is not the leader's personal accomplishment nor a benefit that comes with leadership. The promise was given to the church, that is, the people and the leader. The leader must therefore recognise and encourage the believers to function within their purpose as defined by the Holy Spirit.

In the last days,' God says, 'I will pour out my Spirit upon all people. Your sons and daughters will prophesy. Your young men will see visions, and your old men will dream dreams. **(Acts 2:17)**

The Holy Spirit Fills the Believer

The leader must be filled with the Spirit, a prerequisite for victorious Christian living. The Holy

Spirit provides the directional thrust to move the believer toward obedience to God. As He permeates our lives, He brings the believer under His direct influence, and the character of the Holy Spirit is produced as a result. In the same way, wine dominates the drinker, the influence of the Spirit dominates the life of the person who submits.

Don't be drunk with wine because that will ruin your life. Instead, be filled with the Holy Spirit. **(Ephesians 5:18)**

The Holy Spirit confirms our relationship and status as children of Jesus Christ.

You, however, are not in the flesh but in the Spirit, if in fact the Spirit of God dwells in you. Anyone who does not have the Spirit of Christ does not belong to him. But if Christ is in you, although the body is dead because of sin, the Spirit is life because of righteousness.

(Romans 8:9-10)

The internal witness of the Holy Spirit is vital to the leader's understanding of their positional relationship with Christ. He will confirm and reaffirm our standing. The leader must know to whom he/she belongs and who he/she is. This same Holy Spirit confirms the work of salvation with the leader's life.

The Spirit himself bears witness with our spirit that we are children of God, and if children, then heirs—heirs of God and fellow heirs with Christ, provided we suffer with him in order that we may also be glorified with him.

(Romans 8:16-17)

The Holy Spirit provides both empowerment and fellowship with God. Therefore, the leader must continuously submit to His guidance to enrich his/her life and the lives of those to whom he/she is called to impart.

NOW, WIN AT LEADING

"It is fatal to enter a war without the will to win it."
-General Douglas MacArthur

It is time to turn your attention to the significant ingredients necessary to provide the platform for the leader with a winning mindset to function excellently. Below is a recipe that will affirm, encourage, and empower the leader to serve with distinction.

An energetic leader can inspire others to pursue God's mission selflessly and willingly. The goal of leadership is to create a winning culture by motivating others to discover and fulfill their purpose while effectuating God's mission as set out in the Great Commission.

Therefore, go and make disciples of all the nations, baptizing them in the name of the Father and the Son and the Holy Spirit. Teach these new disciples to obey all the commands I have given you. And be sure of this: I am with you always, even to the end of the age."

(Matthew 28:19-30)

The effective leader must embrace, adopt, and share God's vision to encourage all men to develop a relationship with God.

The Lord isn't really being slow about his promise, as some people think. No, he is being patient for your sake. He does not want anyone to be destroyed but wants everyone to repent. **(2 Peter 3:9)**

The creative leader employs innovative strategies through observation and other research methods and every available medium to propagate the message of the cross.

'Go out into the country lanes and behind the hedges and urge anyone you find to come, so that the house will be full.

(Luke 24:23)

Effective leadership is not about making speeches or being liked; leadership is defined by results not attributes.

<u>(Peter Drucker)</u>

The strong leader serves the mission excellently and considers everything he or she does an opportunity to serve God. He or she plans meticulously, mobilises the strongest team, and executes assignments to bring glory to God. The decisive leader sees an opportunity in every crisis.

And we know that God causes everything to work together for the good of those who love God and are called according to his purpose for them. **(Romans 8:28)**

The wise leader depends on the Lord's leadership and thus constantly engages in prayer.

Trust in the Lord with all your heart; do not depend on your own understanding. Seek his will in all you do, and he will show you which path to take. **(Proverbs 3:5-6)**

The optimistic leader leads others along the route directed by the Lord.

Winning leaders are confident, determined, supportive, and willing to risk it all to please God, knowing that God's promises are sound and can always be relied upon.

The discerning leader depends solely on God, His will, and His Holy Spirit to perfect His will.

The steps of a good man are ordered by the LORD: and he delighteth in his way. **(Psalms 37:23)**

The presence of challenges and adversities serves as motivation to navigate through seasons of failures and losses. The optimistic leader serves God's mission and often takes a calculated risks in the face of danger.

But Moses told the people, "Don't be afraid. Just stand still and watch the Lord rescue you today. The Egyptians you see today will never be seen again. **(Exodus 14:13)**

The selfless leader is willing to submit to God's will and count all previous accomplishments and personal accolades lost to serve God's mission wholeheartedly.

I once thought these things were valuable, but now I consider them worthless because of what Christ has done. Yes, everything else is worthless when compared with the infinite value of knowing Christ Jesus my Lord. For his sake I have discarded everything else, counting it all as garbage, so that I could gain Christ and become one with him. ***(Philippians 3:7-9)***

The winning leader recognises that his/her purpose is to foster a culture of influencing leaders to excel while identifying their own purpose. Therefore, leaders should have a thorough understanding of the purpose they serve, the goals they are seeking to achieve, and the vision they are pursuing. Collectively, these serve as caution signs for informing the team's action.

You can make many plans, but the Lord's purpose will prevail. ***(Proverbs 19:21)***

The winning leader must produce an environment of trust, commitment, integrity, prayer, faith, and knowledge. When we create an atmosphere embodied by love and concern for others, chaos is minimised, and it lays the proper foundation to establish a lasting and meaningful relationship.

Instead, we will speak the truth in love, growing in every way more and more like Christ, who is the head of his body, the church. He makes the whole body fit together perfectly. As each part does its own special work, it helps the other parts grow, so that the whole body is healthy and growing and full of love. **(Ephesians 4:15-16)**

Leaders develop communities in which the opinions, perspectives, and recommendations of others are valued and treated with respect. A community characterised by trust is safe for disseminating critical information, including the overarching plan for the vision. Only in an environment of trust can people grow, expand their knowledge, and freely utilise creativity, skills, and intelligence.

Don't be selfish; don't try to impress others. Be humble, thinking of others as better than yourselves. Don't look out only for your own interests, but take an interest in others, too. **(Philippians 2:3-4)**

Leadership is the capacity to translate vision into reality.

(Warren Bennis)

The fair leader holds others accountable while being accountable to God and others, such as a spouse, children, and other team members. If one attempts to hold others accountable but lives by another standard, such a person is a hypocrite. In Matthew 7, we meet a group of leaders who enforced a standard they were unwilling to live by, and Jesus had these harsh words for them.

"Do not judge others, and you will not be judged. For you will be treated as you treat others. The standard you use in judging is the standard by which you will be judged.

(Matthew 7:1-2)

Leaders think and talk about the solutions. Followers think and talk about the problems. *(Brian Tracy)*

The last chapter is still being written, the gauntlet has been thrown down, and the world is now ready for a generation that will win at leading.

GLOSSARY

Vision: A vision is a mental portrait of a preferable future.

Leader: A person who leads or commands a group, organisation, church, or country.

Administration: The process of operating a group, organisation, or church.

Management: Management also involves organisation achieving objectives with maximum efficiency and responsibility for the result.

Passion: a strong feeling of enthusiasm or excitement for something or about doing something.

Commitment: the state or quality of being dedicated to a cause, activity.

REFERENCE

Leadership Ministry Inc. (2020). What about Biblical Accountability. In *What about Biblical Accountability*. Retrieved from https://leadmin.org/articles/what-about-biblical-accountability

ABOUT THE AUTHOR
Nicholas A Robertson (Director)

NICHOLAS A. ROBERTSON, Dip. Min (Hon.), Dip.Ed. (Hon.), BD (Hon.) B. Ed (Hon.) M.Ed. (Hon.) is a dynamic speaker, counsellor, mentor, and educator who meticulously uses his expertise from military service and his pedagogy to expound on the principles of the Kingdom of God. From as early as 2006, he has been actively involved in ministry and his service transcends borders. To date, he has served in Jamaica, the United States of America, and the United Kingdom. Rev Robertson has operated in the following areas: Youth Ministry, Evangelism, Christian Education, Leadership, Radio, and Social Media ministry.

He studied at the Church Teacher's College, University of the West Indies, Mona, United Theological College of the West Indies, and the Christian Leaders College.

He is the founder of Positive Vibration 365 Plus Global, a daily devotional on social media; co-host of Mr. & Mrs. Robdon's Couples Corner and is also the founder and COO of BuildAMan Foundation Global., a non-profit initiative to develop Godly men, husbands, and fathers. He is also co-founder and director of Impact Online Bible Institute Ltd. He is also the author of Positive Vibration: Navigating through Difficult Times, a book about equipping persons with the appropriate attitude to navigate life's journey. He is also the author of Positive Vibration: Biblical Keys for Faith Activation. Additionally, he co-authors Critical Keys for Biblical Interpretation: The Believer's Handbook (Book 1 and Book 2)

Nicholas 'Robdon' Robertson is married to Danielle Robertson and they both share two beautiful children: Danick and Danice.

ABOUT THE AUTHOR
Valentine Rodney (Deputy Director)

REV. VALENTINE A. RODNEY, BSc, MA. is an international speaker whose ministry has taken him to the USA, Canada, Europe, Africa, and several countries within the Caribbean, where he has also fostered and facilitated ministerial developmental programmes. He has done undergraduate work at the University of the West Indies in Marine Biology and Graduate work in Missions at the Caribbean Graduate School of Theology. Rev. Rodney has served in the areas of Christian Education, Evangelism, Leadership Development, Prayer and Intercession, Youth Ministry, Radio and Television and Pastorate. He is also actively involved in welfare programmes and mentorship to men, youths, and ministers. He is a strong advocate for Christian Transformational Development where the church interfaces with the community and assists in strategic intervention that is both redemptive and empowering.

He is the author of the books, Shameless Persistence the Audacity of Purposeful Praying, La Persistencia Desvergonzada: La Audacia de la Oración con Propósito and The Power of the Secret Place; the place of relationship, resolution, and revelation and has co-authored Critical Keys for Biblical Interpretation: The Believers Handbook (1&2).

Rev. Rodney is an International Instructor for Walk Thru The Bible Ministries, Co-founder and Deputy Director of Impact Online Bible Institute (IOBI), and the Director of Word Impact Ministries International, a non-denominational ministry that caters to the empowerment of the Christian Community and the salvation of the lost. He is an International Chaplain and Ambassador with Covenant International University and Seminary. His Motto is *"Go where there is no path and leave a trail."* VALENTINE A. RODNEY is married to Yevett for twenty-four years and their union has produced two daughters, Zharia and Ana-Olivia.

CONTRIBUTING AUTHOR
Danielle Brown-Robertson (Admin Director)

DANIELLE BROWN-ROBERTSON, BA (Hon.), Post Grad Dip is a dynamic speaker and Educator. Being the child of ministers, she became actively involved in the church in her teenage years and later pursued theological studies at the United Theological College of the West Indies. Prior to migrating to the US, Danielle served as youth minister and administrative secretary for the United Church in Jamaica and the Cayman Islands. Due to her love for nurturing young minds, she completed teacher training at UWI and worked in the middle school classroom in the US. On migrating to the UK, Danielle made a bold decision to decline her teaching role and support the Kingdom inspired vision, Positive Vibration. She is currently the weekly host of the morning program and co-host of Mr and Mrs Robdon Couples' Corner. Along with her husband she leads a family vlog on YouTube called **'THE ROBDONS'** where they provide useful tips on marriage, finances, and family. She has dedicated her time to advance the vision.

Danielle is the wife of Nicholas A Robertson and the mother of two beautiful children, Danick and Danice.

BECOME A STUDENT AT IOBI

We are a subsidiary organization of the Positive Vibration Global group of ministries dedicated to providing training to the community equipping them to serve areas of ministry within the marketplace.

We offer flexible and affordable tailored to you or your church's demand. These include six weeks courses, webinars, accelerated program, training and support programs, life coaching, leadership, and empowerment programs.

Our courses are thoroughly researched and prepared with you in mind.

Follow the link to register: https://bit.ly/IOBIRegistration

ADDITIONAL RESOURCE

Check out our books from varying categories:

Faith, discipline and growth:

Enduring difficult times

Building Thriving Marriages:

Building Thriving Marriages:

Leadership, Administration and Management:

Creating Financial Freedom.

Discipleship, Evangelism, Missions:

Youth empowerment and mentorship:

Purpose, Vision, Leadership, Men Empowerment:

Creating Intimacy in marriage.

Tools for interpreting the Bible:

Tools for interpreting the Bible:

Prayer, reflection, and meditation:

Prayer, reflection, and meditation:

Prayer, reflection, and meditation:

Prayer, reflection, and meditation:

- ✓ **Visit our website to order Sign Copies:** https://www.positivevibrationglobal.com/shop
- ✓ Also available on Amazon and Barnes & Noble
- ✓ Contact us on Facebook @Nicholas-Robdon Robertson
- ✓ Email: nrobertson@positivevibrationglobal.com

Notes

www.ingramcontent.com/pod-product-compliance
Lightning Source LLC
Chambersburg PA
CBHW070642160426
43194CB00009B/1550